Developing
READING AND WRITING
SKILLS

FOR THE YEAR 8 TESTS

DR CHALLONER'S GRAMMAR SCHOOL
AMERSHAM

AD ASTRA PER ASPERA

ear 8 Develop. R + W Skills - Book No. 10

CW00547227

JOHN DAYUS · ANDREW BENNETT

Heinemann

Heinemann Educational Publishers
Halley Court, Jordan Hill, Oxford OX2 8EJ
A division of Reed Educational and Professional Publishing Ltd

OXFORD MELBOURNE AUCKLAND
JOHANNESBURG BLANTYRE GABORONE
IBADAN PORTSMOUTH (NH) USA CHICAGO

Text © John Dayus and Andrew Bennett 2002

The author and publisher gratefully acknowledge Elizabeth Clark for her work in helping with the development of this book.

Copyright notice
All rights reserved. No part of this publication may be reproduced in any material form (including photocopying or storing it in any medium by electronic means and whether or not transiently or incidentally to some other use of this publication) without the prior written permission of the copyright owner, except in accordance with the provisions of the Copyright, Designs and Patents Act 1988 or under the terms of a licence issued by the Copyright Licensing Agency Ltd, 90 Tottenham Court Road, London W1P 0LP. Applications for the copyright owner's written permission to reproduce any part of this publication should be addressed in the first instance to the publisher.

First published 2002
06 05 04 03 02
10 9 8 7 6 5 4 3 2 1

ISBN 0 435 10615 5

Designed and produced by Gecko Ltd, Bicester, Oxon

Printed and bound in Italy by Trento s.r.l.

Original illustrations © Heinemann Educational Publishers 2002

Illustrations by Jan Nesbitt: pages 7, 55, 57, Alice Englander: page 8, Tony Forbes: page 10, Gecko Ltd: pages 5, 38, 47, 50, 53, 62, 64, 88, 109, 123, Kiran Ahmad: page 18, Paul McCaffrey: pages 22, 28, Chris Brown: page 23, Abigail Conway: page 34, John Storey: pages 40–1, 111, 112

Acknowledgements
The authors and publishers would like to thank David Robinson for his work as grammar consultant, which is much appreciated. They would also like to thank the readers and schools at which material was trialled for their invaluable feedback.

The publishers have made every effort to trace the copyright holders, but if they have inadvertently overlooked any, they will be pleased to make the necessary arrangements at the first opportunity.

Extracts: from *The True Story of the Three Little Pigs* by Jon Scieszka. Copyright © 1989 by Jon Scieszka, text. Used by permission of Viking Penguin, an imprint of Penguin Putnam Books for Young Readers, a division of Penguin Putnam Inc.; from *The Three Little Wolves and The Big Bad Pig*. Text copyright © 1993 Eugene Trivizas. Published by Egmont Books Limited and used with permission; from *The Invisible Man* and *The War of The Worlds* by H. G. Wells. Reprinted by permission of A. P. Watt Ltd on behalf of The Literary Executors of the Estate of H. G. Wells; from *The Day of the Triffids* by John Wyndham, published by Penguin Books. Reprinted by permission of David Higham Associates Limited on behalf of the author; from *Brother in the Land* by Robert Swindells, published by Oxford University Press. Reprinted by permission of Oxford University Press; from anecdote about Nelson Mandela, by

Richard Stengel. © Richard Stengel. Reprinted with permission of the author; from *Johnny and the Bomb* by Terry Pratchett. © Terry and Lynn Pratchett 1996. Published by Doubleday, a division of Transworld Publishers. All rights reserved. Reprinted with permission of the publishers; from *X Files 6 – Shapes* by Ellen Steiber, published by HarperCollins Publishers. Reprinted with permission of the publishers; from *Carrie's War* by Nina Bawden (Puffin 1974), Copyright © Nina Bawden, 1973. Reprinted with permission of Penguin Books Limited; from *Stone Cold* by Robert Swindells (Hamish Hamilton, 1993) Copyright © Robert Swindells, 1993. Reprinted by permission of Penguin Books Limited; from *The Outsiders* by S. E. Hinton (Victor Gollancz/Hamish Hamilton 1970) Copyright © S. E. Hinton, 1967. Reprinted by permission of Penguin Books Limited; from www.cdnwriter.com/stories/HorseAndWar.shtml by Lorne Laliberte. © Lorne Laliberte. Reprinted with the kind permission of the author; *Grasshopper Gumbo* from www.lavamind.com/food.html. Reprinted with the kind permission of LavaMind, USA; from www.walks.com. Reprinted with the kind permission of The Original London Walks; *Cassandra talks to you about – The Woman Who Hangs This Morning – Ruth Ellis* from Daily Mirror, 13 July, 1955. Reprinted with permission of The Mirror Syndications; *As Oklahoma bomber Timothy McVeigh is Executed!* From Daily Mail, 12th June, 2001. Reprinted with permission of Atlantic Syndication on behalf of Daily Mail; from Voluntary Euthanasia Society. Reprinted with the kind permission of The Voluntary Euthanasia Society; 'In Mrs. Tilscher's Class' by Carol Ann Duffy from *The Other Country* by Carol Ann Duffy published by Anvil Press Poetry in 1990. Reprinted by permission of Anvil Press Poetry Limited; 'Like A Beacon' by Grace Nichols from *The Fat Black Woman's Poems* published by Virago. Copyright © Grace Nichols. Reproduced with permission of Curtis Brown Ltd, London on behalf of Grace Nichols; 'Immigrants' by Fleur Adcock, from Fleur Adcock, *Poems 1960-2000* published by Bloodaxe Books, 2000. Reprinted by permission of the publishers; from *The Bird's Custard: The True Story* by Nicholas Kurti from *But The Crackling Was Superb: An Anthology of Food and Drink by Fellows and Foreign members of the Royal Society*, Nicholas Kurti, Giana Kurti and Adam Hilger, published by IOP Publishing. Reprinted by permission of IOP Publishing Limited; from *Salt on the Snow* by Rukshana Smith, published by Bodley Head. Used by permission of The Random House Group Limited; from *A Roof Over Your Head* by Bill Naughton, published by Penguin. © Bill Naughton. Reprinted by permission of Peters, Fraser & Dunlop on behalf of The Estate of Bill Naughton; 'Portrait of Machine' by Louis Untermeyer from *Rhyme and Reason*. Published by arrangement with the Estate of Louis Untermeyer, Norma Anchin Untermeyer c/o Professional Publishing Services Company. This permission is expressly granted by Laurence S. Untermeyer; from PC World instore leaflet *Your Guide to our After Sales Service*. Reprinted with the kind permission of PC World, Marketing Dept.

The publishers would like to thank the following for permission to reproduce photographs on the pages noted.
Cover: SUPERSTOCK. Inside: Hulton Archive/Bert Hardy (evacuee, p 47); Terence Spencer/TimePix/Rex features (greaser, p 47); Image State (cup, p 62); Corbis/David and Peter Turnley (gymnasts, p 62); Popperfoto/Reuters (football rioters, p 71); BBC (BBC News at 10, p 73); C5 (C5 news, p 73); Hulton Archive (Travers Symons, p 76); Rex Features/Timepix (suffragette, p 77); Corbis/Bettman (Ruth Ellis, p 82); Rex Features (Timothy McVeigh, p 87); Hulton Getty (school, p 97); Rex Features/Lesley Smith (Caribbean market, p 98); Collections/Gerry Gavigan (beach, p 103); Illustrated London News (Titanic sinking, p 121).

Tel: 01865 888058 www.heinemann.co.uk

Introduction

Developing Reading and Writing Skills has been designed to help you further develop your reading and writing skills throughout Year 8.

It will build on your strengths at word, sentence and text level and pinpoint areas that you need to focus on for improvement. Using this book will help you to make significant progress in English. It will also prepare you for end-of-year assessment and beyond.

Section A develops your understanding of a wide range of fiction and non-fiction texts through exploring their stylistic features. You are then asked to use what you have learned in order to craft your own writing in a range of genres. The objectives for each unit are clearly stated so that you know specifically what you are learning, and the end-of-unit assessments help you to track your progress and to set targets.

Section B gives you guidance and practice in preparation for the optional Year 8 tests, written by one of the leading developers of the tests. It contains:

- *guidance* that will help you to understand what the marker is looking for in different kinds of reading and writing questions, and how you can best respond
- *a diagnostic test* that will help you identify your strengths and weaknesses so that you can set targets and develop your skills
- *a practice reading and writing test* that will help you prepare for the actual test and give you confidence in your skills for end-of-year assessment and beyond.

We hope that you enjoy the variety of activities in the book and in the process develop effective reading and writing skills that you can use across the curriculum.

John Dayus
Andrew Bennett

The following icons are used in this book:

 this is the starter activity   *this is the plenary activity*

 this is the main activity   *there are worksheets to support this activity*

The first three represent the different parts of the lesson structure.

Contents

Introduction 3

Section A

Unit 1 'Something Old, Something New'

1.1 Exploring the narrative style of fairy tales 6
1.2 Telling tales for different audiences 9
1.3 An old tale with new clothes 14
1.4 A message in the tale 16
Reading assignment: *Little Red Riding Hood* 20

Unit 2 Texts from different times

2.1 The changing face of science fiction 22
2.2 The creation of a new world 27
2.3 The future at our fingertips 29
2.4 Future voices 32
Reading assignment: from *Brother in the Land* by Robert Swindells 36

Unit 3 The power of narrative

3.1 I want to tell you a story 38
3.2 The story so far 42
3.3 Write on ... 47
3.4 Write now ... 49
Writing assignment: *Horse* by Lorne Laliberte 52

Unit 4 Instruction, information and persuasion

4.1 Steps one, two and three 54
4.2 A persuasive argument 58
4.3 A style focus 61
4.4 On the trail of ... 64
Writing assignment: Ghostly walks 66

Unit 5 Different styles for different audiences

5.1 Exploring texts and the media 68
5.2 Putting on the style 72
5.3 The art of journalism 76
Reading assignment: Suffragist Outrages 80

Unit 6 Persuasive and argumentative writing

6.1 An age-old argument	82
6.2 A modern debate	86
6.3 Putting a case together	90
6.4 Putting the case	92
Reading assignment: The Case for Voluntary Euthanasia	94

Unit 7 Poetry from different times and cultures

7.1 Painting pictures with words	96
7.2 The best words in the best order	100
7.3 Poetry from your background	103
7.4 Poetry in your words	105
Writing assignment: Fantasy Island	108

Unit 8 In search of the truth

8.1 The making of history	110
8.2 Painting the past with words and pictures	115
8.3 Making a case for history	118
Writing assignment: The *Titanic* Ordeal – a survivor's tale	122

Section B

Preparing for the Year 8 English Test

The reading paper	124
The writing paper	126
Using the diagnostic and practice tests	129

Diagnostic tests

Reading test: from *Bird's Custard: the True Story*; from *Salt on the Snow* by Rukshana Smith	130
Writing test: an argument about food	134

Practice tests

Reading test ('Machines'): Portrait of a Machine by Louis Untermeyer; from *A Roof Over Your Head* by Bill Naughton; *How can we help you* from a PC World leaflet	135
Writing test ('Machines'): March of the machines!	143

A1 'Something Old, Something New'

In this unit you will be developing your skills as an active, critical reader. You will be investigating how writers take familiar material and give it their own particular twist. You will explore how ideas within the *Three Little Pigs* fairy tale are developed in a variety of ways for different effects. Then, having identified these techniques, you will go on to write your own version of a traditional tale for a particular audience.

1.1 Exploring the narrative style of fairy tales

Objectives:
- *developing your skills as an active, critical reader*
- *tracing the development of themes, values and ideas in texts*
- *experimenting with different language choices to imply meaning and to establish the tone of a piece.*

Telling tales

Many stories and folk tales have been passed on from parent to child for generations. Not only are the stories themselves traditional – the way of telling them also follows a familiar pattern. Not only do we know the story-line of the stories themselves, but we are also familiar with the way in which the stories should be told, e.g. how the giant bellows to Jack in *Jack and the Beanstalk* and how Granny responds to the wolf in *Little Red Riding Hood*.

What do we already know about fairy tales?

1 Work in pairs to brainstorm a list of ingredients for a traditional fairy story. To do this, think about:
   - how they start
   - how they finish
   - the characters you meet in fairy tales
   - the language of fairy tales.

   As you think of 'ingredients' for your list, experiment with recipe-style **nouns** to create the language of measurements, e.g. *a **sprinkling** of magic, a **spoonful** of happiness*.

2   Feedback your ideas to the whole class and compile a class list entitled *'The Main Features of a Fairy Tale'*.

 Taking a closer look at tales we know well

3   Read the passage below, which is a 'traditional' opening for *The Three Little Pigs*. As you read the story, check your class 'features list' to see which of your listed 'ingredients' are present in this story opening.

A

Once upon a time there were three little pigs who lived with their mother. One day she told them they were old enough to go out into the world and make a living for themselves. She said, 'Watch out for the big bad wolf, because he will eat you.' She also told them, 'Build your houses nice and
5   strong so that you will be safe from the wolf.' Then she said, 'Good-bye, my sons, and good luck!'

The three little pigs then went their separate ways. The first little pig saw a man stacking straw. The first little pig asked the man, 'May I have some of that straw to build a house?' The man agreed and the first little pig built
10   his house very quickly. It wasn't a very strong house.

One day the big bad wolf came and knocked on the first little pig's door and said, 'Little pig, little pig, let me come in.' And the little pig answered, 'No, no, I won't let you come in, not by the hair on my chinny chin chin.' 'Well,' said the wolf, 'then I'll huff and I'll puff and I'll blow your house in.' So he
15   huffed and he puffed and he blew the house down and ate the little pig.

The second little pig was going along the road when he met a man stacking a big pile of sticks. The second little pig asked the man, 'May I have some of those sticks to build myself a house?'…

4 Look carefully at the last paragraph of the passage. The narrative is similar to that in the second paragraph:

Lines 7–8: The first little pig saw a man stacking straw.

Lines 16–17: The second little pig was going along the road when he met a man stacking a big pile of sticks.

Now look at the **dialogue** of the passage. Identify where the dialogue is similar.

- Note down your ideas on why the author has chosen to repeat similar ideas.
- What do you think is the effect of this technique on the reader?

5 Now re-read the opening section of *The Three Little Pigs*. Remembering that both the narrative and dialogue use repetition as a technique, write the rest of the fourth paragraph. As you are doing this, remember you are trying to *recreate the style* of this author, not just end the story.

6 Next, write the fifth paragraph, still *keeping to the style* of the opening. (You should follow the pattern that has already been laid down in the previous paragraphs to help you to do this.)

Fairy tales often use repetition. For instance, in *Cinderella*, the Prince tries to make the glass slipper fit the foot of different people and there is a strong element of repetition before he finally tries the slipper on the foot of Cinderella.

7 Starting from the moment when the Prince discovers the glass slipper in *Cinderella*, write the ending of this traditional fairy tale. Underline passages where you have repeated ideas for effect.

Tools of the tales!

Look again at the features list you created at the beginning of this section.

8 In pairs, create a 'Top Ten Style Tips' for someone who is about to write a traditional fairy tale. Think about what you have learnt about typical features of fairy tales and about the ways in which they use language.

9 Share your ideas with the rest of the class.

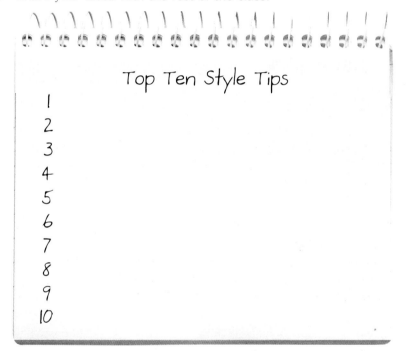

Top Ten Style Tips
1
2
3
4
5
6
7
8
9
10

1.2 Telling tales for different audiences

Objectives:
- *developing your skills as an active, critical reader*
- *identifying ways in which meanings are conveyed in different texts*
- *developing an imaginative or unusual treatment of familiar material.*

Heroes and villains of traditional tales

1 With a partner, brainstorm as many **adjectives** as you can that describe the character and actions of a typical hero or villain, e.g. *evil, cunning, nasty*.

2 Now place these adjectives in a **continuum**, placing the most important at one end and the least important at the other.

3 Which words on your list are **synonyms** – conveying the same meanings?

Bearing your list of **adjectives** in mind, as you read the following adaptations, consider which words and phrases *shape our opinions* on the different characters.

Familiar tales with a twist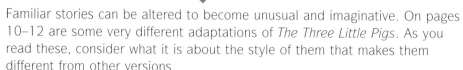

Familiar stories can be altered to become unusual and imaginative. On pages 10–12 are some very different adaptations of *The Three Little Pigs*. As you read these, consider what it is about the style of them that makes them different from other versions.

4 Read text **B** below, and then answer the questions that follow.

B

Everybody knows the story of the Three Little Pigs. Or at least they think they do. But I'll let you in on a little secret. Nobody knows the real story, because nobody has ever heard *my* side of the story.

I'm the wolf. Alexander T. Wolf.

5   You can call me Al.

I don't know how this whole Big Bad Wolf thing got started, but it's all wrong.

Maybe it's because of our diet.

Hey, it's not my fault wolves eat cute little animals like bunnies and sheep and pigs. That's just the way we are. If cheeseburgers were cute, folks

10 would probably think you were Big and Bad, too.

*From **The True Story of the Three Little Pigs** by Jon Scieszka*

a) How does the author create the impression of the wolf addressing the reader directly?

b) Where does the author use informal, even slang expressions? What is the effect of this?

c) What is the effect of the author's deliberate misuse of capital letters towards the end of the passage?

d) How does the author create humour in the piece?

5 Having identified some of the **stylistic conventions** of this piece of writing, now write the next ten lines or so of text B. Remember to use a similar sentence structure and language style to maintain the humour of the passage. Also, don't forget to address your reader directly.

Now read through the very different version of *The Three Little Pigs* in text C, below.

As you read this adaptation of the tale, try to identify how the meaning and ideas in the original version have been developed.

C

So the three little wolves built themselves an extremely strong house. It was the strongest, securest house one could possibly imagine. They felt very relaxed and absolutely safe.

The next day, the big bad pig came prowling along the road as usual. The
5 little wolves were playing hopscotch in the garden. When they saw the big bad pig coming, they ran inside their house, bolted the door and locked all the sixty-seven padlocks.

The pig pressed the video entrance phone and said 'Frightened little wolves with the trembling chins, let me come in!'

10 'No, no, no!' said the little wolves. 'By the hair on our chinny-chin-chins, we will not let you in, not for all the tea leaves in our china teapot!'

'Then I'll huff and I'll puff and I'll blow your house down!' said the pig.

So he huffed and he puffed and he puffed and he huffed, but the house didn't fall down. But the pig wasn't called big and bad for nothing. He
15 brought some dynamite, laid it against the house, lit the fuse and …

the house blew up.

The little wolves just managed to escape with their fluffy tails scorched.

'Something must be wrong with our building materials,' they said. 'We have to try something different. But *what*?'

20 At that moment, they saw a flamingo bird coming along pushing a wheelbarrow full of flowers.

'Please, will you give us some flowers?' asked the little wolves.

'With pleasure,' said the flamingo bird and gave them lots of flowers. So the three little wolves built themselves a house of flowers.

25 One wall was of marigolds, one wall of daffodils, one wall of pink roses and one wall of cherry blossom. The ceiling was made of sunflowers and the floor was a carpet of daisies. They had water lilies in their bathtub and buttercups in their fridge. It was a rather fragile house and it swayed in the wind, but it was very beautiful.

30 Next day, the big bad pig came prowling down the road and saw the house of flowers that the little wolves had built.

He rang the bluebell and said, 'Little frightened wolves with the trembling chins and the scorched tails, let me come in!'

'No, no, no!' said the little wolves. 'By the hair on our chinny-chin-chins,
35 we will not let you in, not for all the tea leaves in our china teapot!'

'Then I'll huff and I'll puff and I'll blow your house down!' said the pig.

But as he took a deep breath, ready to huff and puff, he smelled the soft scent of the flowers. It was fantastic. And because the scent took his breath away, the pig took another breath and then another. Instead of
40 huffing and puffing, he began to sniff.

He sniffed deeper and deeper until he was quite filled with the fragrant scent. His heart became tender and he realised how horrible he had been in the past. In other words, he became a big *good* pig. He started to sing and to dance the tarantella.

45 At first, the three little wolves were a bit worried, thinking that it might be a trick, but soon they realised that the pig had truly changed, so they came running out of the house. They introduced themselves and started playing games with him. First they played pig-pog and then piggy-in-the-middle and when they were all tired, they invited him into the house.

50 They offered him china tea and strawberries and wolfberries, and asked him to stay with them as long as he wanted.

The pig accepted, and they all lived happily together ever after.

From **The Three Little Wolves and The Big Bad Pig** *by Eugene Trivizas*

This adaptation was **parodying** (mimicking) the style of the original fairy tale to create humour.

For instance, instead of:

The big bad wolf came walking down the road frightening the three little pigs.

the author writes:

> *The next day, the <u>big bad pig</u> came prowling along the road as usual. The <u>little wolves were playing hopscotch in the garden</u>.*

Switching the good and bad characters in the tale creates the 'humour'. This is continued throughout the tale.

The use of parody

6 In groups, read through the passage again and make a spider diagram of all the examples of where the conventional ideas from the fairy tale have been swapped around or adapted. Look for words and phrases that you would associate with the fairy tale but which have been used in different ways. It has been started below for you.

The little wolves just managed to escape with their fluffy tails scorched

Mimicking the fairy tail

7 However, the passage also retains much of the traditional language of the fairy tale. Now complete a second spider diagram, this time showing the 'traditional' language of the story in the opening two paragraphs of the passage. Once more, the diagram has been started below for you.

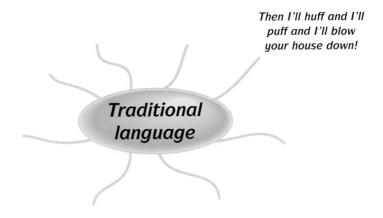

Then I'll huff and I'll puff and I'll blow your house down!

Traditional language

It's a style thing!

8 Look again at texts **A**, **B** and **C**. Fill in a table like the one below, showing where the passages either show the expected 'conventions of a fairy tale' or where they depart from the 'traditional style'.

Different versions of 'The Three Little Pigs'		
Text A	*Text B*	*Text C*
Examples of where this passage displays the 'conventions' of the traditional fairy tale.	Examples of where this passage departs from the fairy tale tradition.	Examples of where this passage departs from the fairy tale tradition.
1		
2		
3		
4		

9 As a class, decide on the *top three features* that are *altered* to create a modern slant on a traditional tale.

1.3 An old tale with new clothes

Objectives:
- *developing your use of commentary and description in narrative by addressing the reader directly*
- *experimenting with different language choices to imply meaning and to establish tone*
- *developing an imaginative treatment of familiar material*
- *recognising how the degree of formality influences word choice.*

In text B, you looked at the story of *The Three Little Pigs* written from a different viewpoint – in this case, that of the wolf. The writer used sentences that were not always grammatically correct to create the effect of addressing the reader directly. It was written as if the wolf was actually talking to *you*, the reader.

When is a sentence not really a sentence?

1 In pairs, re-read text B and pick out the sentences that are not grammatically correct. Discuss why they are not correct and write these points down.

Writing in the style of ...

The passage below was one pupil's attempt to write in the style of text B.

> I will tell you the real story of The Three Little Pigs. They left their homes and built their houses. I was really hungry. I hadn't eaten for nearly a week. So I came across this house of straw and I could hear a pig whistling inside the house.
>
> I called out 'Little pig, little pig, let me come in.'
>
> 'Not by the hairs of my chinny chin chin!' he replied. Therefore, I huffed and I puffed and blew his house in.

2 Still in pairs, discuss the passage above. How far does it succeed in maintaining the tone of text B? Where does it fail to maintain the tone of text B? What advice would you give to the author in order to improve it?

3 Now read the passage below, and when you have done so, discuss how far this succeeds in maintaining the tone of text B.

> So, anyway, it was a Saturday, I think. Cold, and I tell you, I hadn't eaten since Wednesday. Now I ask you, wouldn't you be hungry? I mean, a wolf has to eat. So as I was passing this house of straw, there was this pig – ugly he was – little, spiteful eyes and a sneer on his face – and he was leaning out of his window. I swear he had a death wish.
>
> 'Struttin' your stuff, Wolfie?' he called out to me.
>
> 'Come out here and say that!' I retorted. I was mad now, real mad.
>
> He muttered some garbage about the hairs of his 'chinny chin chin' and I just kicked off. I mean, I've got a short temper anyway, but he got me so mad ...

As you discuss how successful this attempt is, consider the following questions:
- *Is the character of the wolf maintained? If so, how?*
- *Does the wolf still seem to be talking directly to the reader? If so, how is this achieved? (Think about both the language of the passage and the sentence structure.)*
- *How has the writer maintained the humour of text B?*
- *How has the writer maintained elements of the traditional fairy tale?*

4 Discuss your findings with the rest of the class.

 5 Adapting a story in a particular way is referred to as a **treatment** of the tale. Now try to **treat** *one* of the following fairy tales in a similar way.

a) *Hansel and Gretel* from the witch's point of view, or

b) *Little Red Riding Hood* from the wolf's point of view, or

c) *Jack and the Beanstalk* from the giant's point of view.

Remember to try to make the piece humorous and make the villain likeable.

Taking stock – evaluating your writing

6 When you have finished, annotate around your writing in a different colour. Explain what techniques you have tried to use in the writing of this piece and the effects you are hoping to achieve. Try to identify where you have worked hard on creating the idea of the character talking to the reader directly, and also how you have tried to build humour into the piece.

7 Now swap with a partner. How successful is their piece in creating humour through the eyes of the villain?

If you could set one target for them, what would it be?

1.4   A message in the tale

Objectives:
* *developing your skills as an active, critical reader*
* *tracing the development of themes, values or ideas in texts*
* *developing the use of commentary and description in narrative.*

Your Granny would always say ...

In small groups, brainstorm as many different **proverbs** (wise sayings) as you can think of, e.g. *All that glitters is not gold*; *More haste less speed*.

Share your ideas with the rest of the class and discuss why you think we have these sayings and where they came from.

The moral of the tale

Folk tales originate from a particular group of people or community who have passed the story on to their children down through the generations. Although fairy tales show us that evil does not prosper, folk tales often have a more explicit **moral**, which means a 'message', or advice on how people should behave or live their lives.

1 Printed below is a Korean folk tale. Read through the story, and consider, as a group, what you believe the 'moral' of the story to be.

(Note: there is more than one interpretation of the moral of this tale.)

The Tiger in the Trap

Once upon a time, there was a small hamlet in the deep mountains. The people of this hamlet were always afraid of tigers that roamed in the surrounding mountains. One day, their fear and anxiety brought all the villagers together to discuss their problem and find some ways of living
5 peacefully without this constant fear. After much discussion, they came to an agreement: they decided to dig pits here and there to trap tigers. Every able-bodied villager came out to dig deep pits around the village and, particularly, along both sides of the mountain pass leading to the village.

One day, a traveller was passing through the area and heard strange
10 groaning sounds nearby. He approached where the sounds came from and found a large tiger trapped in a pitfall and trying to jump out. Seeing the traveller, the tiger begged him for help: 'Please, help me out of this trap, and I will never forget your kindness.' Out of mercy, the traveller dragged a felled tree and lowered it into the pitfall. And the tiger climbed out.

15 As soon as the tiger was out of the trap, he said to the traveller: 'I am grateful for your help, but because humans made the trap to catch me, for that I will have to kill you.' The traveller was utterly speechless and became frightened, too. Trying to be calm and mustering his courage, however, he said: 'Wait a minute, Mr Tiger. It is patently unfair and
20 outrageous to kill me. Fairness demands that we should have a few impartial parties to judge who is right.' The tiger agreed and both of them went to an ox.

After listening to their story, the ox said: 'Well, it is the fault of humans. We, oxen, too, have a grudge against humans. They drive us hard for their
25 own benefit and then they butcher us mercilessly. This is all very unfair!'

Next, they went to a pine tree. The pine tree listened to their story and said: 'Humans are wrong. They cut us down for lumber and for their firewood. What have we done to them to deserve that? They just have no heart!'

30 Listening to the second opinion, the tiger was elated and ready to attack the traveller, when a hare was hopping toward them. 'Phew, just in time, Mr Hare. Please, judge our case,' and the traveller told the hare what had happened. The hare, then, said: 'Fine, but before I make any judgment, I must see the original scene.' So, the traveller, the tiger and the hare all
35 went to the pitfall where the tiger had been trapped. The hare said to the tiger: 'I must see exactly how you were before this traveller rescued you. Where exactly were you?' Eager to show where he was, the tiger jumped

right into the pitfall. The hare asked: 'Was this felled tree in the pitfall when
you fell into it, Mr Tiger?' 'No, it was not.' So, the hare and the traveller
40 took the tree out of the pitfall. The hare, then, said to the traveller: 'Mr
Traveller, now, be on your way.' And the hare, too, hopped away.

2   We have already discovered that famous sayings are often brief and to
    the point, so now write down the moral of the Korean folk tale in no
    more than *fifteen words*.

3   At the beginning of this unit (page 6), you suggested a number of
    'ingredients' for a fairy tale. Remind yourself what these were, then make
    a table like the one below. On the left-hand side, note down each
    'ingredient', and on the right-hand side, note down whether it can be
    observed in this tale.

Ingredient	'The Tiger in the Trap'
Usually starts with 'Once upon a time'	Once upon a time there was a small hamlet ...

4   As a class, discuss what similarities and differences you have spotted
    between the folk tale and traditional fairy tale? Why do you think this is?

5   Look at the dictionary definition opposite for 'myth', noting the layout
    and style of the entry. Now, write your own dictionary definitions for **folk
    tale** and **fairy tale**.

myth (mith) *noun*
1 a traditional tale, usually about
supernatural beings or events, sometimes
used as an explanation of natural events.
2 a fictitious person or thing.
3 a popular belief: *the myth that women
are worse drivers than men.*
[Greek *mythos* a story]

 6 You have already written an imaginative interpretation of a *well-known*
fairy tale. Now you are going to move forward into writing your own folk
tale or fairy tale, following a traditional pattern.

First, you will need to plan the tale, under the following headings:
- *brief synopsis (outline of the plot)*
- *characters*
- *how the tale will begin*
- *element of repetition*
- *how the story will end (resolution)*
- *the moral of the tale.*

7 Write a first draft of your tale. Like all the tales we have explored, it
should be no longer than 750 words. Remember to use the **conventions**
that make fairy/folk tales different from other kinds of stories.

8 Exchange stories with a partner. You should both consider how far your
partner's tale follows the **conventions** of the fairy/folk tale, and how far
the moral of the tale has been expressed. Having read your partner's
work, give him/her three pieces of advice to improve the work. Think
about language style as well as content.

9 Now redraft your own story. In doing so, try to take into account any
useful advice that you have been given.

Tales – you win!

10 Work in a group of four. Tell a brief tale about what you have learned in
your work on section 1.4, using the stylistic conventions of fairy tales.
Each member of the group should begin his/her section of the tale with
the following phrases:
- Once upon a time four friends called **, **, ** and ** were ...
- They learned all about ... (four or five things)
- They especially learned ... (the single, most important thing)
- They all decided to ... and lived happily ever after.

Reading assignment

This test is 40 minutes long

- *You should spend the first 5–10 minutes reading the text and questions carefully before you start writing your answers.*
- *Looking at the marks for each question helps you to judge how much to write for each answer.*

Little Red Riding Hood

Wance upoan a time there wis a wee lassie called Agnes, but she aye wore a wee coat wi a red hood her Mammy bought her at the market so folk aye called her Little Red Riding Hood. But we're different so we're goanny call her Agnes.

5 Agnes had a granny who lived in a wee pensioner's flat just roond the corner fae her hoose. Wan day granny goat awfy sick an Agnes's Mammy told her tae take some food an a bottle o gin to her. So Agnes pit oan her wee coat an took the shopping trolley her Mammy hid put aw the stuff in an set af tae her Granny's flat.

10 So there Agnes wis, skippin alang an sining a wee song. She wis so happy that she didnae notice the wolf who wis walking ahind her. Noo this wolf wus known in the area fer likin tae eat auld grannies, nay idea why but wolves are strange anyway an we didnae write this story in the first place!

Noo the wolf happened tae know Agnes an her Granny so he worked oot
15 that's where she wis headin. So he ran oan in front o her an goat tae Granny's flat afore Agnes did. He knocked oan the door an Granny got oot of bed tae answer it. Well, it were surprise she goat tae see a big wolf stawnin there, well ye didnae see many o them in Castlemilk dae ye?

The wolf pushed Granny intae the flat and tied her up wi a pair o old
20 laddered tights he found sittin oan the chair. Then he loacked her in her wardrobe efter he pit sticky tape ower her mooth tae stop her yellin....He would have eaten her then an then but he hid just had a curry an wisnae that hungry, so he wis savin her fur his supper.

Then alang came Agnes who didnae knoak oan the door as it wis her
25 Granny's hoos efter aw. She went intae the bedroom an there wis the wolf lyin oan the bed wearing her Granny's flannelette nightie an her wee wooly bed soaks.

Noo Agnes wisnae that bright an couldnae see it wis a wolf an no her Granny lyin there but she did think Granny looked an awfy colour an there
30 wis something different aboot her.

'Oh Granny wit big eyes ye huv,' she said.

'Aw the better tae see ye wi,' said the wolf.

'Oh Granny wit big ears ye huv,' she said.

'Aw the better tae hear ye wi,' said the wolf.

35 'Oh Granny wit big teeth ye huv,' she said.

'Aw the better tae eat ye wi,' said the wolf and he jumped oot o the bed, grabbed Agnes and tried tae eat her but of course he hid just had that curry an noo it wis beginnin tae tell oan him.

The noise he wis makin (no tae mention the smell) alerted aw the
40 neighbours who came rushin in tae see where the party wis an how come they werny invited. The wolf goat such a fright he ran oot the flat, doon the road an never went back tae that street again. Granny wis let oot o the wardrobe 2 days later when everywan had finished her food an gin.

Agnes is grown up noo an works fer a wolf rehabilitation program in
45 Callendar … so some good came oot o that day.

1 Where did Granny live?

[1 mark]

2 What do we learn about Granny's lifestyle?

[2 marks]

3 Why didn't the wolf eat her?

[1 mark]

4 Where does the writer give the impression he is speaking directly to an audience?

[2 marks]

5 What traditional fairy tale elements have been retained in the story?

[3 marks]

6 Where has the author adapted this to make it a more 'modern' tale? Refer to two or three particular parts in answering the question.

[2 marks]

7 Which ideas, words and phrases have helped the author to make the story amusing?

[4 marks]

8 This version of 'Little Red Riding Hood' has not been written for small children, but instead for a more grown-up audience. How do we know this?
You should write about:
• the choice of language
• the description of the characters
• the ending.

[5 marks]

In this unit you will be exploring differences between texts written in different times, specifically investigating extracts from the science fiction genre through the years. You will explore how authors create mood and atmosphere in science fiction, and how the texts reflect the time in which they were written. Then you can go on to create your own science fiction text.

2.1   The changing face of science fiction

Objectives:

- *recognising the conventions of science fiction writing*
- *identifying the social contexts of stories from different ages*
- *recognising how texts refer to and reflect the culture in which they were produced*
- *identifying the ways in which meanings are conveyed in text.*

The land of make believe?

The art of **science fiction** writing is to develop ideas, making imaginative use of scientific knowledge, and to explore the unknown. Readers are encouraged to believe these things could happen one day in the future. As science becomes more advanced, so science fiction becomes more imaginative.

1   Look at the list opposite. It includes elements from science fiction stories throughout the years. With a partner, think about advances in scientific knowledge. Try to put them in order, showing when they may have occurred in science fiction writing, starting with the earliest and moving through to the most recent.

- UFOs
- 'designing' people at conception
- space travel
- creating poisons, weapons for mass destruction
- transplants of parts of the body
- creating a computer system that knows everything about you
- travelling through time
- cloning
- ability to 'teleport'
- ability to read minds and thoughts of others.

2 Now share your findings with the rest of the class. How many of the 'fictions' have become reality?

From this world to the next

The passage over the next two pages is by H.G. Wells. It is the ending of his story *The Invisible Man*, and was written in 1897. In this scene, the invisible man has been surrounded by a frightened crowd and beaten to death. As he dies, he begins to lose his invisibility.

3 As you read the passage, consider how the tension of the situation is created.

In another second there was a simultaneous rush upon the struggle, and a stranger coming into the road suddenly might have thought an exceptionally savage game of Rugby football was in progress. And there was no shouting after Kemp's cry—only a sound of blows and feet and a
5 heavy breathing.

Then came a mighty effort, and the Invisible Man threw off a couple of his antagonists and rose to his knees. Kemp clung to him in front like a hound to a stag, and a dozen hands gripped, clutched, and tore at the Unseen. The tram conductor **suddenly** got the neck and shoulders and lugged him back.

10 Down went the heap of struggling men again and rolled over. There was, I am afraid, some savage kicking. Then suddenly a wild scream of 'Mercy! Mercy!' that died down **swiftly** to a sound like choking.

'Get back, you fools!' cried the muffled voice of Kemp, and there was a vigourous shoving back of stalwart forms. 'He's hurt, I tell you. Stand back!'

15 There was a brief struggle to clear a space, and then the circle of eager eyes saw the doctor kneeling, as it seemed, fifteen inches in the air, and holding invisible arms to the ground. Behind him a constable gripped invisible ankles.

'Don't you leave go of en,' cried the big navvy, holding a bloodstained
20 spade; 'he's shamming.'

'He's not shamming,' said the doctor, **cautiously** raising his knee; 'and I'll hold him.' His face was bruised and already going red; he spoke **thickly** because of a bleeding lip. He released one hand and seemed to be feeling at the face. 'The mouth's all wet,' he said. And then, 'Good God!'

25 He stood up **abruptly** and then knelt down on the ground by the side of the thing unseen. There was a pushing and shuffling, a sound of heavy feet as fresh people turned up to increase the pressure of the crowd. People now were coming out of the houses. The doors of the Jolly Cricketers were suddenly wide open. Very little was said.

30 Kemp felt about, his hand seeming to pass through empty air. 'He's not breathing,' he said, and then, 'I can't feel his heart. His side – ugh!'

Suddenly an old woman, peering under the arm of the big navvy, screamed sharply. 'Looky there!' she said, and thrust out a wrinkled finger.

And looking where she pointed, every one saw, faint and transparent as
35 though it was made of glass, so that veins and arteries and bones and nerves could be distinguished, the outline of a hand, a hand limp and prone. It grew clouded and opaque even as they stared.

'Hullo!' cried the constable. 'Here's his feet a-showing!'

And so, **slowly**, beginning at his hands and feet and creeping along his
40 limbs to the vital centres of his body, that strange change continued. It was like the slow spreading of a poison. First came the little white nerves, a hazy grey sketch of a limb, then the glassy bones and intricate arteries, then the flesh and skin, first a faint fogginess, and then growing **rapidly** dense and opaque. **Presently** they could see his crushed chest and his
45 shoulders, and the dim outline of his drawn and battered features.

When at last the crowd made way for Kemp to stand erect, there lay, naked and pitiful on the ground, the bruised and broken body of a young man about thirty. His hair and beard were white – not grey with age but white with the whiteness of albinism, and his eyes were like garnets. His
50 hands were clenched, his eyes wide open, and his expression was one of anger and dismay.

'Cover his face!' said a man. 'For Gawd's sake, cover that face!' and three little children, pushing forward through the crowd, were **suddenly** twisted round and sent packing off again.

55 Someone brought a sheet from the Jolly Cricketers, and having covered him, they carried him into that house.

*From **The Invisible Man** by H. G. Wells*

*One of the ways in which H. G. Wells engages his reader in the action of the story is by the use of adverbs. Some of these are in **bold** font in the passage.*
*Remember that an **adverb** is a word that modifies a **verb**.*
*e.g. to walk **slowly***
*   to **quietly** weep.*

4   Skim the passage, and in each case, identify the verb that each adverb refers to. The first one has been done for you.

Adverb	Verb
suddenly	got

5   Now go back to the adverbs that are in bold font in the passage. Using a range of **antonyms**, (opposites), replace the adverbs so that the actions in the passage are described in a very different way.

6   When you have completed this activity, think about why the author used the particular adverbs he did, and then write a sentence to explain each of the following:
   a) the effect of the adverbs *suddenly* and *swiftly* in lines 9 and 12
   b) the effect of the adverb *cautiously* in line 21
   c) the effect of the adverb *slowly* in line 39
   d) the effect of the adverb *rapidly* in line 43.

Try to use the words **pace** and **mood** to show how the author builds up atmosphere in the passage.

From ordinary to extraordinary and fantastic

Another way in which H. G. Wells engages his audience is by mixing images that are very **familiar** to us, very **ordinary** and very ***English***, with images that are **fantastic** or **strange**.

The struggle described in the first paragraph of the extract from *The Invisible Man* is compared with a very English, ordinary image of a *game of Rugby football*. Yet, in the midst of the struggle is the **fantastic**, **extraordinary** image of a dozen hands tearing at *the Unseen* – the invisible man.

This mixing of the ordinary and extraordinary can be seen below, in a short extract from another of H. G. Wells's science fiction stories, *The War of the Worlds*.

> *A big greyish, rounded bulk, the size, perhaps, of a bear, was rising slowly and painfully out of the cylinder. As it bulged up and caught the light, it glistened like wet leather. Two large dark-coloured eyes were regarding me steadfastly. It was rounded, and had, one might say, a face.*

7 Clearly, this is an extraordinary and terrifying moment, but what words and phrases can you pick out of the passage that could be described as 'normal' and 'matter of fact'?

8 How can using *ordinary* images be more effective in building up tension than, for instance, shouts and screams of terror?

WS 9 Read through the passage from *The Invisible Man* again. Now draw up a table like the one that has been started below. List as many **strange** or **fantastic** images as you can. Alongside each image, explain how it contributes to the build-up of tension. Then do the same with the images that are very English or normal.

Fantastic or strange image	*Effect of image on reader*	*Traditional English or commonplace image*	*Effect of image on reader*
A dozen hands tore, gripped, clutched and tore at the Unseen.	The reader can imagine many people apparently grappling with nothing. The use of the words the Unseen adds more mystery	... might have thought an exceptionally savage game of Rugby football was in progress.	Rugby football is a typically English game and the reader is encouraged to think of a rugby scrum at this point. Also the phrase exceptionally savage is the voice of a calm narrator.
		Kemp clung to him in front like a hound to a stag	

Caught in the act

10 Now in groups, create a tableau (freeze-frame) of any part of the story, showing the contrast of the 'fantastic' and 'commonplace' building up the tension of the moment.

As you show your tableau to the rest of the class, one member of your group should take the part of the director and explain the images caught in your freeze-frame. Try to explain how each individual in the group contributes to the image created.

2.2 The creation of a new world

Objectives:
- *identifying the ways in which meanings are conveyed in text*
- *analysing the overall structure of a text to identify how key ideas are developed, particularly through patterns of language used*
- *exploring the impact of a variety of sentence structures.*

Sinister beginnings

1 Read the short extract below. The author is describing the moment when the Invisible Man becomes visible. The two sentences work well with each other because one is very detailed and one is short and to the point. Together they create a sinister picture.

> And so, slowly, beginning at his hands and feet and creeping along his limbs to the vital centres of his body, that strange change continued. It was like the slow spreading of a poison.

2 Now, with a partner and using some of the words below, write two sentences describing the sighting of a strange creature. Try to create a sinister mood.

evil, piercing, shimmering, breathless, horrific, glimpse, creature, strange, lumbering

Share your ideas with the class. Which words from the list are more effective at creating the sinister mood? Why?

 3 Draw up a class 'dictionary' of different **adjectives** and **adverbs** you would expect to find in a good piece of science fiction writing. You need to list the words and also explain what they mean and the mood they create.

Spinning a web of intrigue

Now let us look more closely at the whole paragraph that describes the 'fantastic' scene of the Invisible Man slowly becoming visible:

*And so, slowly, beginning at his hands and feet and creeping along his limbs to the vital centres of his body, that strange change continued. It was like the slow spreading of a poison. First came the **little white** nerves, a hazy grey sketch of a limb, then the **glassy** bones and intricate arteries, then the flesh and skin, first a faint fogginess, and then growing rapidly dense and opaque. Presently they could see his crushed chest and his shoulders, and the dim outline of his drawn and battered features.*

The author develops the sense of the 'fantastic' and incredible, particularly by his use of sentence structure. The same passage has been printed below as separate phrases.

And so, slowly,
beginning at his hands and feet
and creeping along his limbs to the vital centres of his body,
that strange change continued.
It was like the slow spreading of a poison.
First came the little white nerves,
a hazy grey sketch of a limb,
then the glassy bones and intricate arteries,
then the flesh and skin,
first a faint fogginess,
and then growing rapidly dense and opaque.
Presently they could see his crushed chest and his shoulders,
and the dim outline of his drawn and battered features.

4 Study the passage as it has been laid out at the bottom of page 28. Now use this to help you to answer the questions below.

   a) Which **words** does the author use to link **phrases** and give a sense of the passage of time?

   b) How does the **language** he chooses help the author emphasise the **slowness** of the strange change?

   c) What is the effect of the **simile** *It was like the slow spreading of a poison* in the middle of the passage?

   d) You will see that the author often separates phrases by using **commas**. What is the **effect** of this on the passage as a whole?

5 Now, using a large sheet of paper, draw a spider diagram with the title 'Developing atmosphere in science fiction writing'.

   With this title in the centre, show in your diagram what **skills** and **techniques** a writer would have to use when developing a piece of science fiction writing.

6 With a partner, write one paragraph of a science fiction story, using some of the skills and techniques in your diagram.

7 When you have completed your paragraph, annotate it to show which techniques you have used.

Spielberg move over

8 Now share your paragraph with the class: explain which techniques you have used and why, and explain the overall effect you have achieved.

2.3   The future at our fingertips

Objectives:
- *developing the use of commentary and description in narrative*
- *experimenting with different language choices help to establish 'tone' or atmosphere*
- *experimenting with figurative language in conveying a sense of character and setting.*

From chaos to order

On the next page are some extracts from *The Day of the Triffids*, by John Wyndham (published in 1951). The author is describing London some time after a meteor shower has occurred. This meteor shower has blinded most of the population and civilisation is in chaos.

1   The passages are not in the right order. With a partner, decide which sections should go where to create an effective order for this piece of description.

A

It was difficult to believe that all that meant nothing any more, that now it was just a pretentious confection in uncertain stone which could decay in peace.

B

He was sitting close to Lincoln's statue, and clutching to him his dearest possession – a side of bacon from which he was hacking a ragged slice with a blunt knife.

C

The roofs could in due course fall; there would be none to stop them, and none to care.

D

Above it all rose the Houses of Parliament, with the hands of the clock stopped at three minutes past six.

E

And so I came to Westminster.

F

Very few people were in sight. I saw only three who were moving. Two were tapping their way down the gutters of Whitehall; the third was in Parliament Square.

G

Let it shower its crumbling pinnacles on to the terrace as it would – there would be no more indignant members complaining of the risk to their valuable lives.

H

The deadness, the finish of it all, was italicized there. The usual scatter of abandoned vehicles lay about the streets.

I

Alongside, the Thames flowed imperturbably on. So it would flow until the day the Embankments crumbled and the water spread out and Westminster became once more an island in a marsh.

*From **The Day of the Triffids** by John Wyndham*

2 Feedback your ideas to the rest of the class. Which words and phrases helped you decide on the order?

3 Now look at the passage in the correct order as Wyndham wrote it. Which version is more effective, and why?

 A different world

4 Like H. G. Wells, it was said of Wyndham that he liked to mix fantastic images with commonplace images. List the fantastic images that he brings to the reader's attention in the passage.

5 Now imagine what would have happened in the village, town or city where you live. List the landmarks of the place. These could be offices, shops, public houses, sports stadia, etc.

6 Then, write a paragraph in which you describe the changes that have occurred, as in the example given below:

> And so I came to Charles Street. I saw Mrs Bennet's sweet shop. I had spent much of my childhood in there. Now the window was shattered and the shelves had been stripped bare. The till was full of money. Nobody had bothered to steal it; there was no use for money any more. People would steal a loaf of bread before they stole a million pounds.
> Further up, moss was growing on the memorial to the soldiers of the two wars. Their names were still there, but for how long? There was now nobody to look upon it, nobody to leave flowers in remembrance...

7 Next, introduce one or two characters to your piece of writing. Where will they be? What will they look like? What will they be doing? Use the passage from *The Day of the Triffids* and the example below for ideas.

> On the grass beside the memorial sat a young girl of about fifteen. Her face was grey with grime, and she wore the ragged remains of what, at one time, would have been a pretty, blue flowery dress. In her hand was a tin which she was smashing angrily against a stone in an attempt to open it ...

8 Complete your writing by adding further paragraphs, each paragraph dealing with another 'landmark' listed in question 5. You might also add another character or two to help to develop the atmosphere of your writing.

Countdown and evaluate

9 Pick out a detail of your story that you are particularly pleased with. Explain in just one minute why you like it, and what it shows you have learned about science fiction writing.

2.4 Future voices

Objectives:
- *developing the use of commentary and description in narrative*
- *experimenting with different language choices to help establish 'tone' or atmosphere*
- *experimenting with figurative language in conveying a sense of character and setting.*

A garden of verbs

The passage opposite is taken from *The Day of the Triffids*. In it, Wyndham describes the scene in a village on the south coast of England six years later. Bill, the narrator, is with his girlfriend, Josella. They are noticing how seaside villas are disappearing under a mass of vegetation.

The passage has been set out to enable you to focus on particular words and phrases.

Grass and weeds had a good hold in the gutters
and were <u>choking</u> the drains.

Leaves had <u>blocked</u> downspoutings
so that more grass,
5 and even small bushes,
<u>grew</u> in cracks
and the silt of the roof gutterings.

Almost every building was beginning to <u>wear</u> a green wig,
beneath which its walls would damply rot ...

10 The gardens of the Parks and Squares were wildernesses
<u>creeping</u> out across the bordering streets.

Growing things seemed, indeed,
to <u>press</u> out everywhere,
<u>rooting</u> in the crevices between the paving stones,
15 <u>springing</u> from cracks in concrete,
<u>finding</u> lodgements even in the seats of the abandoned cars.

On all sides they were <u>encroaching</u> to repossess themselves of the arid
spaces that man had created....

'Only so few years ago,' Josella <u>said</u> reflectively, 'people were <u>wailing</u>
20 about the way those bungalows were <u>destroying</u> the countryside. Now
look at them.'

'The countryside is having its revenge, all right,' I said. 'Nature seemed
about finished then – who would have thought the old man had so much
blood left in him.'

From **The Day of the Triffids** by John Wyndham

1 With a partner, select all the underlined verbs and replace them with
   your own choice.
2 How has the change of verbs affected the tone of the description?

Writing the future

3 Look carefully at the construction of the sentences in the passage on page 33.

   a) How has the author separated the phrases in this piece of writing?

   b) What is the effect of this technique?

   c) What does this passage have in common with the passage from *The Invisible Man* in terms of the sentence structure?

4 Now look again at your own piece of writing. Experiment with your own sentence structure to produce a similar 'tone' in your own writing.

5 Now look at the dialogue at the end of the passage from *The Day of the Triffids*. It might be said that this captures the 'theme' or message of the book: that nature is having its revenge on mankind, who has destroyed so much of nature in the past.

6 Once more, try to introduce some dialogue into your own writing. The characters that you have described earlier could be given dialogue, or perhaps you might speak as the narrator.

The example below shows how dialogue and description can be woven together to create a particular mood.

On the grass beside the memorial sat a young girl of about fifteen. Her face was grey with grime, and she wore the ragged remains of what, at one time, would have been a pretty, blue flowery dress. In her hand was a tin which she was smashing
5 angrily against a stone in an attempt to open it.

I approached her carefully. 'Let me open that for you,' I said. She jerked upright, obviously afraid, and hugged the tin protectively to her chest. Her eyes looked blindly in my direction. 'It's alright, I don't want your tin. It's a tin of
10 prunes, by the way. Do you like prunes?'

'How do you know?' she asked.

'Know what?'

'What's in the tin. Can you see?'

'Yes.'

10 She scrabbled backwards on the grass. 'Please don't take it off me,' she pleaded. 'Please don't ...'

A world of difference

7   Working in a group, list five key questions you would ask when considering the effectiveness of a piece of science fiction writing. The first one has been done for you.
    a) When was this piece written? How do I know this?
    b)
    c)
    d)
    e)

8   Now apply these questions to your own writing.

9   What aspect of your writing needs developing for you to be as effective as Wells and Wyndham?

Reading assignment

This test is 40 minutes long

- *You should spend the first 5–10 minutes reading the text and questions carefully before you start writing your answers.*
- *Looking at the marks for each question helps you to judge how much to write for each answer.*

The passage below is taken from Robert Swindells' *Brother in the Land*. The author is describing a town in the days following a nuclear attack.

On the edge of town the houses were all burnt out, charred, glassless windows and caved-in roofs. Inside you could see wallpaper, fireplaces and bits of stairs going nowhere. Smoke rose thinly here and there through the blackened timbers.

5   There was this old man, sitting in an armchair on the pavement. How it got there I don't know but there he was, staring at the wet flags. He was the first living person I'd seen all the way down and I crossed over and said, 'Are you all right?' It was a damn stupid thing to say but I wanted to hear his voice.

He didn't answer. He didn't even look up. He just went on staring at the
10 pavement with his hands curled round the ends of the armrests. I repeated my question in a louder voice but there was no response; not even when I touched his shoulder. I guessed he must be in shock or something and I felt I ought to help – get him under cover, perhaps. I looked about but all the houses were burnt and I couldn't see anybody else, so I left him.

15 As I moved further into the town the damage got worse. Some of the buildings had collapsed; drifts of smashed brick lay spilled across the road and I had to pick my way round them. There were more bodies, and broken glass everywhere, some of it fused by heat into fantastic shapes. There were burnt out vehicles and the air smelt of charred wood.

20 Our shop was in the west part of town, the part farthest away from Branford. The worst devastation was to the east. As I made my way westward the damage grew lighter and I began to hope that I might find my family unscathed and my home intact.

I saw people. Some were walking about. Others sat on steps, gazing at
25 the ground in front of them. Nobody looked at me, or tried to speak. I felt invisible, like a ghost.

Treading carefully between heaps of rubble and bits of glass I came to the top of my own street. Some of the houses still stood, others lay smashed. I could see from here that the shop was down.

30 I ran, in the middle of the road. My legs were weak with fear so that I almost fell.

The van lay on its side in the roadway, burnt out. The whole shop had collapsed though nearby houses still stood. I scrabbled among the rubble, calling brokenly to my parents. I imagined them lying crushed or burned

35 beneath the bricks and plaster and I started to dig with my bare hands; pulling out bricks and throwing them aside. Then a voice said, 'Danny?' and I spun round, still bent over with a brick in either hand. My dad was standing by the cellar-steps, looking at me …

*From **Brother in the Land** by Robert Swindells*

1 What was the narrator of the story hoping that he would find?

[1 mark]

2 What image is created by the man sitting in his armchair on the pavement?

[2 marks]

3 Why do you think the old man did not answer the narrator?

[2 marks]

4 What caused the narrator to 'feel invisible'?

[2 marks]

5 What does the author refer to with 'drifts of smashed brick'? How does this build on the image created?

[2 marks]

6 What words/phrases does the author use to suggest that the destruction can also appear quite beautiful?

[1 mark]

7 Explain the effect of the following words:
   a) spilled (line 16)
   b) scrabbled (line 33)
   c) brokenly (line 34)

[3 marks]

8 What is the effect of the 'colloquial' expressions – (those nearer to everyday speech) in this piece of writing?

[2 marks]

9 How does the writer raise the tension over the course of the passage? In your answer, you should consider the:
   • details that have been presented to the reader
   • the language that the author has used
   • and the sentence structure used in the piece of writing.

[5 marks]

In this unit, you will be developing your skills as an active, critical reader and investigating the development of themes, values and ideas in a range of narrative texts.

You will be identifying how key ideas and structures are developed within these texts and then go on to experiment with different approaches to planning and drafting writing, experimenting with different language choices as you write.

3.1   I want to tell you a story

Objectives:

- *identifying ways in which implicit and explicit meanings are conveyed in texts*
- *identifying the key alterations made to a text when it is changed from an informal to a formal text*
- *recognising how the degree of formality influences word choice.*

Words, words, words

1   Look at the list of words below and see how many **synonyms** (words with the same meaning) you can come up with. Try to include some more **colloquial** (informal/familiar) words too.

drink, happy, food, good, bad, pretty, ugly

E.g.:

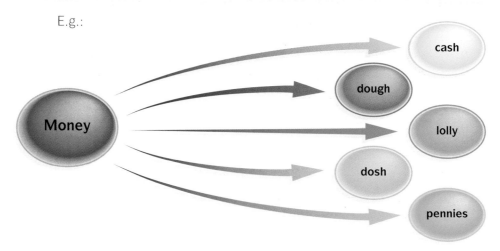

2   Feedback your ideas to the rest of the class. When would you be more likely to use the more colloquial words? Why?

Storytellers of our time

3 Read the passage below. It is an anecdote (a short story about a remembered incident) by Richard Stengel, and is about Nelson Mandela, the former South African president.

A

We were once on this airplane flight down in Natal, and it was a prop plane. I think there were six seats in it, and there were maybe four of us on the plane. And as soon as he gets on an airplane he picks up a newspaper. He adores newspapers. He didn't have them for so many
5 years and he revels in the touch of them, and he reads every stupid story. And so we were sitting on the airplane, the plane was up, and he is reading his newspaper, and we're about, I don't know, halfway there … I was sitting right across from him, and he pointed out the window … and I saw, to my great horror, that the propeller had stopped going around. And
10 he said very, very calmly, 'Richard, you might want to inform the pilot that the propeller isn't working.' I said, 'Yes, Madiba.' I walked to the front of the plane, and the pilot was well aware of it and he said, 'Go back and sit down. We've called the airport. They have the ambulances out there, and they're going to coat the runway with foam or whatever they do.'

15 I went back and I told Madiba that, and he just, in that very solemn way, mouth sort of down, listened, and said, 'Yes.' And then picked up his newspaper and started reading. I was terrified, and the way I calmed myself was I looked at him. And he was as calm as could be. Like the prisoners on Robben Island must have looked at him when they felt
20 scared, and he just looked as calm as could be.

The plane landed, no problem. He never changed his expression or anything like that. He put his newspaper down, and we came into the airport, and as we got into the airport and we sort of had a moment alone, he turned to me and he said, 'Man, I was scared up there.' It was
25 such a revelation because that's what courage is. Courage is not, not being scared. Courage is being terrified and not showing it.

From an interview with Richard Stengel by John Carlin

One way in which we can recognise that the passage was originally a spoken story is the author's use of **colloquial language**. For instance:

I think there were six seats in it, and there were maybe four of us on the plane.

And he was as calm as could be.

If this was written in a more **formal** style, then it could be written like this:

> *There were four of us on a six-seater plane.*
>
> *He was extremely calm.*

4 Which words and phrases would have to be changed if this was to be a piece of text written down in Stengel's memoirs instead of a spoken text?

Write down the colloquial expression, and alongside, write down a formal version of the word, phrase or sentence.

5 Although the story is written down for you, how do you know this story was originally 'spoken' not written down? Think about:

a) the layout of dialogue

b) the use of tense

c) sentence structure.

Writers of fiction do not always write in a formal style, however. Sometimes, they will deliberately write in a colloquial style, to help convey the 'voice' of the narrator.

ws **6** The passage below is taken from the opening of Robert Swindells' *Stone Cold*. When you have read it, answer the questions below.

B

> You can call me Link. It's not my name, but it's what I say when anybody asks, which isn't often. I'm invisible, see? One of the invisible people. Right now I'm sitting in a doorway watching the passers-by. They avoid looking at me. They're afraid I want something they've got, and they're
> 5 right. Also, they don't want to think about me. They don't like reminding I exist. Me, and those like me. We're living proof that everything's not all right and we make the place untidy.

Hang about and I'll tell you the story of my fascinating life.

My fascinating life. Yes.

10 Born March 20th, 1977, in Bradford, Yorkshire to Mr & Mrs X. We were a family, you know – as happy as most, till Dad ran off with a receptionist in 1991, when I was fourteen and at the local comp. This mucked up my school work for quite a while, but that's not why I ended up like this. No. Vincent's to blame for that. Good old Vince. Mum's boyfriend. You should 15 see him. I mean, Mum's no Kylie Minogue – but Vincent. He's about fifty for a start …

*From **Stone Cold** by Robert Swindells*

a) Give three examples of the writer using **colloquial language**, such as: This mucked up my school work …

b) The passage is partly written in the **past tense**, and partly in the **present tense**. Give two examples of each. When does the author use the past tense, and when does he use the present?

c) Give three examples of the author punctuating **phrases** as if they are **sentences**, e.g. Me, and those like me.

d) Give three examples where the narrator seems to be talking **directly** to the reader.

7 Now look again at texts **A** and **B**. As we read both, the narrator is **explicit** about (makes clear) some of his thoughts, and we are left to imagine the **implicit** ideas, although there are clues in the text to help us do this.

Using the grid below, list the implicit suggestions, noting down the clues that lead us to these. One has been done for you already:

Implicit suggestions in Stengel's text	Evidence	Implicit suggestions in Swindell's text	Evidence
Plane is very small passenger aircraft and therefore maybe not as safe as larger aircraft.	I think there were six seats in it, and there were maybe four of us on the plane.	No one is bothered about Link	It's not my name, but it's what I say when anybody asks, which isn't often.

Saying what you mean ... or not?

8 When you have completed the activity, write a paragraph about an incident in your life, where you use **colloquial** expressions and include **implicit** information, as well as **explicit** information.

9 Now write a short paragraph to explain the **effect** of these techniques on the **tone** of the passage as a whole.

3.2 The story so far

Objectives:
- *appreciating the impact of figurative language in texts*
- *analysing how ideas are developed through the patterns of language used*
- *integrating evidence into writing to support analysis.*

The life and soul of the story

Writers often use **adjectives** and **adjectival phrases** to help to bring a passage to life, enabling the reader to picture the scene that the author is presenting.

Remember that an adjective is a word that describes, or qualifies a noun.

Sometimes, a **single adjective** is used, as in *made the cobbles* **slippery**.

Sometimes, a writer uses **more than one adjective**, as in **strange**, **greenish** *tint*.

This collects adjectives together into an **adjectival phrase** to help him/her to describe a setting, a character or a feeling, as in **black night** *sky*.

1 Look at the lists of adjectives and nouns below. With a partner, try to link up pairs or groups of adjectives into adjectival phrases. Then see if you can join these up with a noun that they could describe.

Note, when an adjectival phrase is joined with a noun, it is referred to as a **noun phrase**.

Adjectives

Nouns

drink   streets   weather   storm   fire   eyes
day   sunshine   rain   tree   atmosphere

2 Share your ideas with the rest of the class. Which noun phrases were the most unusual?

Painting the picture

Read the two passages below, which are both openings from novels, and then complete the activity that follows.

A

It was nine o'clock in the evening, in Blackbury High Street.

It was dark, with occasional light from the full moon behind streamers of worn-out cloud. The wind was from the south-west and there had been another thunderstorm, which freshened the air and made the
5   cobbles slippery.

A policeman moved, very slowly and sedately, along the street.

Here and there, if someone was very close, they might have seen the faintest line of light around a blacked-out window. From within came the quiet sounds of people living their lives – the muffled notes of a piano as
10   someone practised scales, over and over again, and the murmur and occasional burst of laughter from the wireless.

*From **Johnny and the Bomb** by Terry Pratchett*

B

Jim Parker had felt the storm building all day. The cattle had been restless that afternoon. The sun had set with a strange greenish tint. Now darkness had fallen, and the wind was up, howling like a man in pain. For the past hour, thunder had been rolling through the Montana skies. The
5   rain hadn't hit yet. But it was coming.

Parker and his son, Lyle, stood inside by the door of the ranch house. They didn't speak. Instead they listened to the sounds of the storm. They were waiting for something. The thing that neither one of them had ever talked about. The thing that came to the ranch to kill.

10   Outside, lightning turned the black night sky to a silver white. As if lightning had split open the clouds, rain began to fall in great windy sheets. And then the house went dark.

*From **The X-Files 6 – Shapes** by Ellen Steiber*

3 Look carefully at the two passages, and complete the table identifying the noun phrases.

Johnny and the Bomb			The X-Files	
Adjectives/Adjectival phrases	Noun modified		Adjectives/Adjectival phrases	Noun modified
occasional				tint
	moon			night sky
	window		silver white	
quiet				
muffled				
	laughter			
occasional				

From the table above, it would appear that *Johnny and the Bomb* is the more descriptive of the two passages. However, *The X-Files* makes much use of **figurative language**. This means the use of a metaphor or simile to create a particular image or mood.

When using a **metaphor**, a writer writes about something as if it were really something else, e.g. *Jenny faced the brick wall of her brother*.

When using a **simile**, the writer creates an image in the reader's mind by comparing one thing with another; a simile contains the word *like* or the word *as* in order to draw the comparison, e.g. *John ate like a horse and was as strong as an ox*.

4 Find **three** examples of figurative language in *The X-Files*. In each case, explain whether the author is using a simile or a metaphor.

5 Then explain briefly what your examples do to develop the tone and mood of the passage.

6 Now compare the two authors' uses of sentences. Which author uses mostly short, simple sentences, and which uses longer, more complex sentences? What effect does this have on the mood of each passage?

The writers in the dock ⬥

7 The passage on the next page shows you how to comment on an author's choice of language and the effect this has on the reader. However, some of the text has been missed out. Work in pairs to try to complete all the missing elements.

The X-Files

In this passage, the writer seems to be intending to scare the reader.

One of the main characters, Jim Parker, is introduced immediately, though we are told nothing about him. Instead, the writer concentrates on developing the setting. The reader is told of the gathering storm. Strange images, such as the cattle growing '①', and the '②' of the sunset add a supernatural sense to Steiber's description.

The description of the sounds of the thunder and the wind 'howling like a man in pain' further adds to the sense of menace. The portrayal of the wind as a human in agony is particularly frightening, I feel. At the end of the first paragraph, the last two sentences should really be written like this: 'The rain ③'. However, the full stop after 'yet' lengthens the pause, and makes the oncoming rain very threatening.

The reader is now waiting for something to happen, especially as the writer uses ④ which produce a series of pauses: 'They didn't speak. Instead they listened to the sounds of the storm.'

The last two sentences of the paragraph start with the words 'The thing', and this repetition emphasises ⑤

In the final paragraph, the imagery becomes violent, surely hinting at more violence that seems likely to follow: '⑥'

Finally, the writer plunges the scene into darkness, the suddenness of this emphasised by ⑦

Start by explaining the intention of the writing.

*Explains the **imagery** that is used by the author. This is **supported** by **examples from the passage**. There is nothing on **character** here, but you would normally include this in your discussion, if it were appropriate.*

*Notice that the writer is giving a **personal opinion** of a particular **simile** here, and there is a comment also about **sentence structure**. Once more, views are supported by **specific examples**.*

*Again, throughout this section, **viewpoints** on **language** and **imagery** are supported by the **quotation** of brief examples from the passage.*

*Notice how the writer is always offering a viewpoint about the text; **never merely retelling the text**, or paraphrasing it.*

***Quotations** are put inside quotation marks, and text is quoted **exactly**.*

8　Now re-read *The X-Files* passage and write a short paragraph where you comment on the kind of images the author is trying to create and the effect language used.

Write and tell

9　With a partner, look back over the points that were made in the 'teaching boxes' alongside the 'model answer' opposite. List the main things a budding writer would have to remember if they were trying to create vivid images in their writing.

3.3　Write on ...

Objectives:
- *experimenting with different approaches to planning and drafting writing*
- *writing a review of a text*
- *experimenting with different language choices to establish tone.*

What's in a picture?

1　With a partner, study both pictures. What words would you use to describe the images created in these pictures?

2　Feedback ideas to the rest of the group, explaining why you think this.

From pictures to words

3　Next, still working as a pair, read both passages printed on the next page. Read the passages aloud to each other, emphasising the words you think are most effective at creating the images within the text.

A

They all seemed to have more luggage than when they had started. Suitcases that had once been quite light now felt as if they were weighed down with stones. And got heavier as they left the small station and straggled down a steep, cinder path. Carrie had Nick's case as well as her
5   own and a carrier bag with a broken string handle. She tucked it under one arm but it kept slipping backwards and her gas mask banged her knee as she walked …

… Nick's hands tightened in hers. She looked at his white face and the traces of sick round his mouth and wanted to shake him. No one would
10 take home a boy who looked like that, so pale and delicate. They would think he was bound to get ill and be a trouble to them. She said in a low, fierce voice, 'Why don't you smile and look nice,' and he blinked with surprise looking so small and so sweet that she softened. She said, 'Oh, it's all right, I'm not cross, I won't leave you.'

*From **Carrie's War** by Nina Bawden*

B

When I stepped out into the bright sunlight from the darkness of the movie house, I had only two things on my mind: Paul Newman and a ride home. I was wishing I looked like Paul Newman – he looks tough and I don't – but I guess my own looks aren't so bad. I have light-brown, almost red hair and
5   greenish-grey eyes. I wish they were more grey, because I hate most guys that have green eyes, but I have to be content with what I have. My hair is longer than a lot of boys wear theirs, squared off in back and long at the front and sides, but I am a greaser and most of my neighbourhood rarely bothers to get a haircut. Besides, I look better with long hair.

10 I had a long walk home and no company, but I usually lone it anyway, for no reason except that I like to watch movies undisturbed so I can get into them and live them with the actors. When I see a movie with someone, it's kind of uncomfortable, like having someone read your book over your shoulder …

*From **The Outsiders** by S. E. Hinton*

4 Once more working in pairs, think through what points you would make about what images are created in the passages, and which words and phrases are most effective. Make a list of your points, remembering to find evidence from the text to support the points you wish to make.

WS 5 When you have completed the preparation work with a partner, work by yourself and write out your 'commentary' of one of the passages. (Use the example on *The X-Files* to remind you how to do this.)

Remember to **paragraph** your work as you explain your viewpoints, as this will help the reader to understand your piece of writing more easily.

6   At the start of this unit, you read out text A or text B to a partner, concentrating on particular words and phrases. Now that you have studied it more closely, you should have a clearer idea of what the writer was trying to achieve. Pick out **two** things that you feel could be reflected in a 'reading' of the passage, e.g. *fear*, *annoyance*, *insecurity*. Tell your partner what they are, then give another reading of the passage.

7   Listen carefully to your partner's reading and comment on how well they have managed to convey the points they have chosen.

From words to pictures

8   With a partner, look again at the two pictures you studied earlier. Using ideas from the two passages, what words would you add to your list to describe the images created in the pictures?

9   Feedback ideas to the rest of the group, explaining your ideas.

3.4   Write now ...

Objectives:

- *experimenting with different approaches to planning and drafting writing*
- *writing a review of a text*
- *experimenting with different language choices to establish tone*
- *experimenting with figurative language.*

Stop here

Below is another passage from Robert Swindells' *Stone Cold*. Sentence boundaries have been removed from the passage.

1   Working in pairs, read the passage aloud to each other, pausing **for effect** where you think it is best to do so. When you have both done this, discuss where you think the full stops would be most effective.

You will find that the text can be broken up into short phrases in places, rather than full sentences.

> I had a hundred and fifty quid on me when I got off the train at King's Cross it was what was left of my savings, plus a twenty Carole slipped me when Chris wasn't looking a hundred and fifty doesn't sound bad does it it sounded okay to me my plan was, I'd get a room somewhere nothing
> 5   posh a bedsit, and then I'd look for work again, nothing posh I'd take anything for a start, just till I established myself and could look round properly I was dead green, see a babe in arms.

2 When you have finished the exercise, prepare a couple of sentences to answer this question:

> **If an editor insisted on Robert Swindells using full sentence structures throughout, what would be the effect on his narrative?**

Bursting to write (ws)

3 Re-read each of the three passages: *Stone Cold*, *Carrie's War* and *The Outsiders*.

4 Now, working as a group, list the main points you have discovered about the style of the writing in one of the passages. Think about:

a) the images created

b) the sentence style

c) the punctuation used.

For instance, if you look again at the extract from *The X-Files*, you might brainstorm the main features of the writing as:

> Focuses on setting
>
> Much detail about the contrast of darkness and light
>
> Refers to sounds as well as sights
>
> Many short sentences and lots of pauses
>
> Use of repetition to emphasise fear

5 Feedback your list to the rest of the class and listen carefully to the points made about the other passages.

6 Now try to bring together the ideas on your list above into a 'short burst' of writing of your own. It might look something like the attempt opposite. Don't worry at this stage if there are crossings out. You will be experimenting with a few ideas and reworking ideas as you write.

Then there was silence. ~~This was followed~~ by a low hissing from beneath the window. Lightning flashed in the sky again in a blood red sky. The ~~hissing grew~~, became a horrible moan threatening, angry ~~growl. It was~~ waiting, waiting for them, warning them. Thunder rolled over them again, echoing across the valley. And then the rain.

To begin with, write just the next ten lines in the style of the passage you have studied.

7   Once you have worked on your own passage, use other groups' ideas about style and write the next ten lines of the other two passages.

Ideas that just grow and grow and grow

8   You should now have three 'short burst' extracts that you have written. Your final task is to expand **one** of these this into a 'sustained' piece of writing.

> **REMEMBER:**
> * *Make sure that you take the main features of the extract into your own writing.*
> * *Draft your work first. This will enable you to experiment with your writing.*
> * *Paragraph your writing.*
> * *Make sure that your final draft is as accurate as you can make it.*

The best of the best

9   Read out your 'best bit' – no more than two or three lines – to the others in your group. Then say why you liked it, and what you did to make it 'fit in' with the style of the original piece of writing.

Writing assignment

Minor task: you should spend about 25 minutes answering this question.

Your writing will be marked for:
- *Your choice and use of vocabulary (4 marks)*
- *How you structure and punctuate sentences and organise paragraphs (4 marks)*
- *The overall impact of your writing on the reader (12 marks)*

Read the following extract from *Horse* – an opening to a first draft of a fantasy story by Canadian writer Lorne Laliberte.

Horse

'I said get off that horse,' the voice repeated, 'and I meant get off that horse now.'

I peered into the bushes about me but still could not determine the source of my troubles. Nor, for that matter, had I any way of knowing what number of companions this stranger could have ...

Now continue writing the next three or four paragraphs of the opening to this fantasy story in your own words.

Remember you only have three or four paragraphs so plan your writing carefully. You are just trying to capture the intended 'mood' of the piece of writing, to develop the scene and the character's from the author's 'story seeds', not to write the whole story. Therefore don't worry too much about the ending.

Use a planning format like the one below to help you plan your ideas before you begin to write.

In this unit you will be exploring how some texts combine instructions with information and persuasion. You will investigate how these texts use language for different effects, and how they build up a picture in the reader's mind. You will then go on to create your informative and persuasive text, combining the genres in one text.

4.1 Steps one, two and three

Objectives:

- *recognising how texts are shaped by the technology they use*
- *developing different ways of linking paragraphs, using a range of strategies to improve cohesion and coherence*
- *extending the range of prepositions and connectives used to indicate purpose.*

I command you to …

Verbs that give straightforward orders or commands are called **imperative verbs**.

1 With a partner, brainstorm all the imperative verbs you might find in a recipe, e.g. *chop*, *mix*.

Because these words instruct you to do something, they are sometimes referred to as *command verbs*.

2 Now list all the command verbs you have heard today, e.g. *sit*.

3 Next make a list of all the places where you would expect to hear or see command verbs, e.g. *school*.

To begin at the very beginning

4 Look at the recipe for Grasshopper Gumbo. The instructions for making this dish have been mixed up. Read through the mixed-up instructions and ingredients and try to put them in the right order.

5 Discuss your order with the rest of the class. How did you work it out?

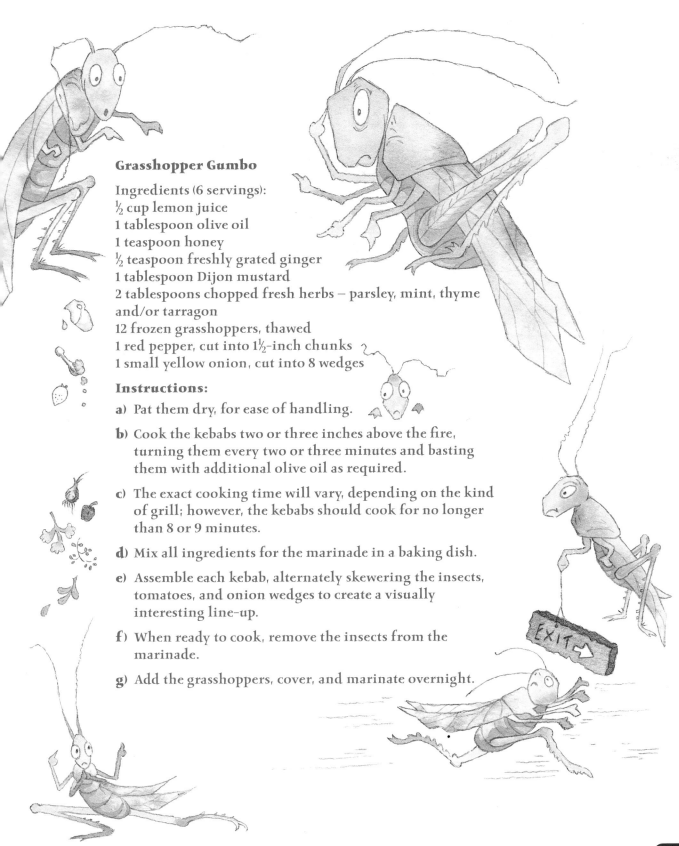

Grasshopper Gumbo

Ingredients (6 servings):
½ cup lemon juice
1 tablespoon olive oil
1 teaspoon honey
½ teaspoon freshly grated ginger
1 tablespoon Dijon mustard
2 tablespoons chopped fresh herbs – parsley, mint, thyme and/or tarragon
12 frozen grasshoppers, thawed
1 red pepper, cut into 1½-inch chunks
1 small yellow onion, cut into 8 wedges

Instructions:

a) Pat them dry, for ease of handling.

b) Cook the kebabs two or three inches above the fire, turning them every two or three minutes and basting them with additional olive oil as required.

c) The exact cooking time will vary, depending on the kind of grill; however, the kebabs should cook for no longer than 8 or 9 minutes.

d) Mix all ingredients for the marinade in a baking dish.

e) Assemble each kebab, alternately skewering the insects, tomatoes, and onion wedges to create a visually interesting line-up.

f) When ready to cook, remove the insects from the marinade.

g) Add the grasshoppers, cover, and marinate overnight.

You could probably work out the order, just from using your knowledge about cooking. However, some instructions need markers to signal a sequence through. These are known as **connectives**.

6 Look at the list of connectives below. Which connectives could be matched with different stages of your re-ordered Grasshopper Gumbo recipe?

next, finally, then, first, now, before, when, after

In some instructional texts, although many sentences begin with command verbs, occasionally, sentences begin with a **preposition**.

Prepositions often indicate **time**:
As *you go through the door, notice the stained glass window ...*

They can also indicate **position**:
At *the junction, take a left turn.*

And they can also indicate **direction**:
Go **through** *the gate; cross over the bridge.*

7 Now rewrite the Grasshopper Gumbo recipe instructions, adding prepositions and connectives.

8 When you have finished, examine your recipe with a partner. What differences has adding these words made to the recipe?

9 Now make a note of other places where you might find instructional writing.

Instructions with a twist

10 Now look at the printout of the web page opposite, giving information about Ghost Walks in London.
Although much of this text is informative and even persuasive, there are still some clear instructions. What are they?

11 How do the instructions on the web page differ from the instructions in the recipe? Why do you think this is?

The Original
LONDON WALKS

Summer 2001 (March 15 – October 31)   "London Walks was the first and is the best of the walking tour firms"
Fodor's Great Britain

► Home
► Contact Us
► Reviews

► Timetable
► Monday
► Tuesday
► Wednesday
► Thursday
► Friday
► Saturday
► Sunday
► Explorer Days

► Private Walks
► Special Walks
► Other Trips

► The Guides
► Questions
► Latest News
► Books
► The Potpourri
► Links

GHOSTS OF THE WEST END
7:30 pm Embankment Underground
⊖ Circle, **Bakerloo**, District & **Northern** ⊖

Tonight we're going to open London's X-files. Venture down shadowy side streets and gas-lit alleys in pursuit of the paranormal. Weave our way into the West End's rich tapestry of strange happenings: everything from the Man in Grey to the Strangler Jacket to Jack Lemmon's brush with the supernatural. Perchance you'll see the headless woman in moonlit St. James's Park. You'll certainly see the most haunted statue in London. And here's a thought: experts say perhaps as many as half the people you see on the streets of London are ghosts! But take heart, after the walk we'll renew our courage in a superb old Georgian pub. But if one of the regulars tells you he's been coming there forever...well, you never know...he just might be telling the truth!

This walk takes place every Monday and Thursday at 7:30pm.

☞ Guided by <u>Graham</u> on Mondays
☞ Guided by <u>Peter</u> on Thursdays

© 2001 <u>The Original London Walks</u> PO Box 1708 London NW6 4LW
Tel: 020 7624 3978 Fax: 020 7625 1932

Find a walk
Enter one or more key words, and or select a day of the week and press go to search the site.

Any day ▼

Go

<u>Click here</u> for detailed search tips.

Site design by
<u>media sterling limited</u>

 ## Getting the picture

12 Quickly, without showing your partner, sketch a very simple picture, like a doodle.

13 Now, using no more than ten steps, give your partner very clear step-by-step instructions for sketching your picture.

14 Now review your pictures. Which one is the nearer to the original? What conclusions could you draw about the instructions given?

4.2   A persuasive argument

Objectives:
- *giving written advice which offers alternatives and takes account of the possible consequences*
- *exploring the effects of changes in tense*
- *understanding and using key terms that help to describe and analyse language.*

Defining moments

1   Look at the words listed below. They are all contained in the leaflet you will be studying. Some of them may be unfamiliar, so look up their definitions in a dictionary and note them down.

Be prepared to explain in your own words what each word means.

raddled, sodden, gore, stealthy, steely, abyss, lour, menacing

Show me, tell me, convince me!

2   Read through the extract from a leaflet detailing the main attractions of the Jack the Ripper Walk.

As you read, think about which words and phrases are designed to **inform** the reader about things they will see, and which are designed to **persuade** the reader to go on the walk.

3   Now re-read the extract, this time noting down in a table as shown below, which particular words and phrases are designed to **inform** the reader about things they will see, and which are designed to **persuade** the reader to go on the walk.

Informative words and phrases	Persuasive words and phrases

Jack the Ripper

He came silently out of the midnight shadows of August 31, 1888, striking terror at the hearts - and throats - of raddled, drink-
5 sodden East End prostitutes and leaving a trail of blood and gore that led … nowhere. *Jack the Ripper!* We evoke that autumn of gaslight and fog, of menacing
10 shadows and stealthy footsteps as we inspect the murder sites, sift through the evidence - in all its gory detail - and get to grips, so to speak, with the main suspects.
15 En route we'll steady our nerves in The Ten Bells, the pub where the victims - *perhaps under the steely gaze of the Ripper himself* - tried to forget the waking nightmare …

20 … *This is the original - and complete - Jack the Ripper Walk.* It begins at Tower Hill, right on the boundary between Scotland Yard territory and City of London Police territory.
25 Only by beginning there can you understand the conflict between the two London police forces and their leading personalities. A conflict which blurred the
30 investigation and made it easier for the Ripper to slip through the police nets.

And please *tread carefully and keep away from the shadows … for you*
35 *are about to enter the abyss.* Which is by way of saying, the setting itself couldn't be more dramatic. Two minutes into the walk a back alley takes us into a hideaway
40 where the grim old London Wall rears up directly before us. It's a hideaway so dark and so still that you can hear people breathing, a place where the clock seems
45 permanently turned back to 1888, back to the *Autumn of Terror.*

Furthermore … This is the only nightly Ripper walk that goes into the spooky old Victorian pub where
50 one of the Ripper's victims drank. Very little has changed … right down to the chilling, old photographs and newspaper headlines that lour at you from the
55 walls. *Here, the autumn of 1888 never ended …*

Don't worry, at the end of the walk you won't have to make the long trek through dark empty streets all
60 the way back to Tower Hill. Our walk ends right at the safe, convenient London Underground station that is very close to where the ghastly murder took place.

From The Original London Walks leaflet - 'Jack the Ripper'

4 Do any words and phrases fit into both columns? Why do you think this is?

One of the things to notice about this type of writing is that both the persuasive and the informative elements tend to include **noun phrases** where images are clearly and vividly depicted.

For instance: *chilling, old photographs*
a hideaway so dark and so still

5 Skim-read through the extract and note down the noun phrases used to create the atmosphere of 1888.

6 Choose a noun phrase that you think is particularly effective and explain to a partner why you like it.

Tense and tension – a winning duo!

7 Identify in the passage where the author uses the past, present and future tenses. When you have done this, answer the following questions:
  a) When does the author tend to use the past tense? Why?
  b) When does the author tend to use the present or the future tense? Why?
  c) Are there any exceptions to the pattern you have identified? What is the effect of this?

8 Now look in a little more detail at the choice of verbs. List the verbs that you think are used to create a particular atmosphere.

9 Which other verbs could have been used instead?

10 How might a change of verbs affect the overall impact of the leaflet?

11 Now, imagine you are going to give advice to a writer on the key elements for success when writing a leaflet that both informs and persuades.
  a) First, note down your main ideas.
  b) Then put them in order, with the most important features first.
  c) Finally, write your advice, explaining why the features you have picked out are important to the overall impact of the piece. The first sentence is written below to start you off:

> When writing a leaflet which offers information but which also wants to persuade the reader to take advantage of an offer, it is essential to remember the following points:
>
> First ...

The judge's decision

12 Now, swap your writing with a partner and read through their piece of advice for writing this kind of leaflet. Put a tick next to all the things you agree with, and a question mark against ideas you have not included yourself or you don't think are essential.

13 Finally, set your partner one target for improving their piece of advice.

4.3　A style focus

Objectives:

- *organising and presenting information, guiding a reader through a text*
- *explaining complex ideas and information clearly*
- *presenting a case persuasively.*

Which way now?

1 List as many imperative (command) verbs as you can think of, that would be useful in giving people directions. The list has been begun for you below.

　　turn, take, proceed

2 Next, make a list of **prepositions** (indicators of time, position, direction) for the same type of writing. These can be used at any point in a sentence, but they are particularly useful at the beginning, to avoid beginning every sentence with a command verb. Again, the list has been begun for you.

　　At the end … Near the … On the left …

3 As a class, collect together these examples for use later.

The way to go

As well as informing and persuading readers, leaflets can also give instructions to follow a route or trail. This is where the use of imperative verbs and prepositions is essential.

4 As you read the extract from a school trail leaflet on page 62, focus both on the verbs used and on the descriptive elements within it that aim to both inform and persuade the readers.

Take the short corridor on your right from the welcome desk. Turn left at the end of the corridor and proceed for about ten metres. On your right, you will see the sports trophy cabinet. Pride of place goes to the beautifully carved Midlands Netball Championship Shield, which our school has won for the last three years. The tall silver cup on its right is the Under-15 cricket championship trophy, and you will also see many inter-house trophies on display.

Continue down the corridor for another twenty metres, and then enter the gymnasium through the blue doors on the right. Every half an hour, you will see our brilliant gymnastics team being put through its paces in a dazzling gymnastic display.

5   Now look at the map below.

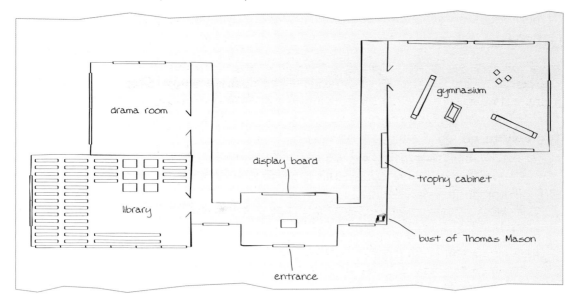

You will see that there are two other rooms to guide people to, and there are two further objects of interest in the school corridor.

You have spoken to various people, and have made the notes displayed below.

6 Complete the information leaflet about this floor of the school, using these notes, and your knowledge of how to write an informative and persuasive leaflet with clear directions.

1 Drama room. Year 10 drama group presenting their own play. School history of drama. Performed at Kilby Arts Festival for last three years. Inter-house drama competition every year.

3 Library. Open an hour before school and an hour after. Full-time librarian. Pupils work in there during lunch hour. Houses 12,000 books - internet access- CD RoMs.

2 Bust of Thomas Mason - engineer, who founded the school in 1867. Cast in bronze. Free school for all the children of Kilby.

4 Display board - photographs of presentation day. Ms S. Harding, chair of Kilby County Council, presenting prizes to winners. Prizes for effort and attainment in every subject; sports prizes; prizes for achievement in working for others.

Desired destination?

7 When you have finished, share your piece of writing with a partner. ***Together***, consider the following questions **for each piece of writing**:

a) Where exactly have you used the conventions that we have explored in this section? (Command verbs, prepositions, appropriate use of tense).

b) Would the reader be able to follow your instructions to find the points of interest? If not, what would you need to alter? (Refer back to the map when checking this).

c) Have you tried to use descriptive language to **persuade** your audience?

8 Now, make a list of no more than five key points you need to remember when you are crafting this type of writing in the future.

4.4 On the trail of …

Objectives:
- *organising and presenting information, guiding a reader through a text*
- *explaining complex ideas and information clearly*
- *presenting a case persuasively*
- *re-reading work to anticipate the effect on the reader and revising style and structure, as well as accuracy with this in mind.*

A mind full of ideas

In this section you will be writing your own trail leaflet.

First, spend a few minutes thinking what it will be about, for example:

Your school
You could write a trail leaflet for an open evening, in which you give parents of primary school children information about the school. In the leaflet, you would draw their attention to important displays and demonstrations, notice boards, works of art, etc.

Your town or village
This could be a general tourist leaflet, pointing out buildings of interest or areas of beauty. Perhaps someone famous lived near you. You could point out where he/she was born, went to school, and where he/she worked.

Something else?
You might have a completely different idea for a trail. (You could have a mystery tour trail or a horror/ghost trail, or you might like to do a 'through the keyhole' leaflet on your home.)

1 Create a mind map of associated ideas you could include. An example of a mind map is shown below.

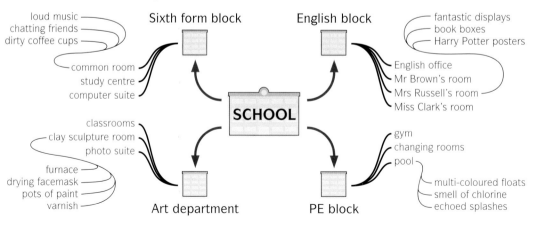

2 Feedback your ideas to the rest of the class.

Great plans

3 When you have decided on your trail, make a table like the one below. Complete the boxes of the table, using the prompts that are there to help you plan your trail leaflet in more detail.

What kind of trail will you write about?	*Route*
	• What route will your trail take? • If your trail is around your village or town, do you expect people to walk or drive? (This will affect how you write your instructions.)
Points of interest	*Presentation*
• How many points of interest will you include in your trail? • What will they be? • How much information will you give about each one? • Will you need to find any information? If so, how will you go about finding out?	• How will you present your leaflet? • What size will it be? • Will you use a camera? • A digital camera? • A word processor? • A desktop publisher? • If so, how will these be used? • Can you get photographs (or photocopies) from the local library? • Can you illustrate your trail yourself?

4 Now, draw up your first couple of paragraphs for your trail leaflet.

5 Then, reading through your leaflet so far, check to see if you have remembered the rules of this type of writing.

> **REMEMBER:**
> *Your leaflet should:*
> • *inform and persuade your audience*
> • *give your audience clear directions.*

6 Now complete your writing, ensuring that your leaflet is informative, persuasive and gives clear directions.

The final stages

7 Now go back to the five key points you devised to help you with this type of writing. Check your first draft against these points and make any amendments necessary when redrafting.

Writing assignment

Minor task: you should spend about 25 minutes answering this question.

> **Your writing will be marked for:**
> - *Your choice and use of vocabulary (4 marks)*
> - *How you structure and punctuate sentences and organise paragraphs (4 marks)*
> - *The overall impact of your writing on the reader (12 marks)*

Read the extract below, which is taken from a website advertising tours/walks around places of historical interest in London.

> ## DRACULA – THE WALK
>
> 7:45 pm Embankment Underground
>
> He is here. London, heart of the Empire in 1897, shelters the blackest heart of all, a creature of the night, the Prince of Darkness. Having duped a London solicitor into assisting him, he has come from his Carpathian lair in Transylvania to sup on blood ... young English blood. You might think yourself safe in this great city, but against a being who can assume any shape, no-one is safe. He must not live! Join Professor Van Helsing or Mina Harker and help track him down ... even unto his sinister old mansion, still there after all these years. And who knows what it might entomb, what might be stirring there even now ... anticipating your arrival. Do bring your own garlic.

Now imagine that you are planning to advertise a new 'ghostly walk' on this web site.

Write the full text for your web page, using the Dracula one above as a model.

- Remember to use appropriate language, tense and sentence structure.
- Don't forget that your writing needs both to inform, and **persuade** your audience of the enjoyment to be gained on the walk.

Remember to plan your writing carefully before you start to write.
You could use a planning grid like the one below:

Words and phrases to describe the atmosphere of the walk	Places of interest on the walk	Words and phrases to describe these places

In this unit you will be investigating how meanings are changed when information is presented in different media and exploring how texts are shaped by the technology they use. You will explore the changing face of reports from newspapers to TV and examine how texts reflect the culture in which they were produced. You will examine a range of reports from different ages and once you have established the features necessary to write an effective report, you will go on to create your own report for a chosen medium.

5.1 Exploring texts and the media

Objectives:
- *investigating how meanings are changed when information is presented in different media*
- *investigating how texts are shaped by the technology they use.*

Reporting the facts

The opening of a report is highly structured, following particular rules, whether it appears in a newspaper, on the Internet, or in a television bulletin.

The opening section of a report will always answer these questions:

- **What?** What has happened, what is the situation, etc.
- **Who?** Who is or was involved.
- **When?** When the event took place, or is likely to take place.
- **Where?** Where the event took place.

A report may then go on to explain:

- **How?** How the event happened. This may include some description of actions.
- **Why?** Why the event took place.

The last two questions, however, may not always be addressed in the very opening stages of a report.

To capture the audience

1   Read through the following openings to reports. Make a table like the one below, and indicate how the **What? Who? When? Where?** questions are answered in each case. The first one has been done for you.

A

> Over £10,000 of computer equipment was stolen from Byte Size computer store in Kilby last night. The owner, Mr Eric Jones …

B

> Two pupils from Fair Oaks Primary School in Nottingham were presented with awards for bravery on Friday.

C

> Passengers at Greenwich Station were left bewildered yesterday morning when the 8.05 train to London sailed straight through the station as part of a time-saving experiment.

D

> An explosion at a paint factory in Leicester on Monday evening resulted in the deaths of two of the workforce …

E

> Ipswich Town's win against Manchester City at Maine Road has swept them into the Premiership top three. As Saturday's results came in, Ipswich manager …

Passage	*What?*	*Who?*	*When?*	*Where?*
A	Computer equipment stolen	From Eric Jones (owner)	Last night	Byte Size computer store, Kilby

2   With the exception of C, none of the opening sentences suggests why the events happened. Brainstorm reasons for this and then feedback ideas to the rest of the class.

Playing to the audience

As we have seen from the extracts above, whatever the audience, the **structure** of the opening to a report will be similar. However, the **style** of the report will vary according to the audience.

3 Look back at the extracts from reports and suggest where you think you might find this kind of report, e.g. *TV news, newspaper, Internet, radio*.

4 Now read the two reports below. They are transcripts from early-morning television news bulletins. When you have read them, consider the questions that follow.

News Hour

Five football fans are being treated in hospital in Barcelona after being stabbed before England's World Cup qualifier match in the city last night. None of them has suffered serious injuries. They were hurt in clashes with rival fans, which occurred on the streets outside the football stadium.
5 Another fan is recovering from being stabbed in the arm the previous day. England won the match 2-0.

The stabbings happened in scuffles outside the newly rebuilt 'state of the art' stadium just minutes before kick-off. Stones and bottles were hurled at the police, and vehicles were set alight as tensions ignited.

10 One English fan was slashed across the chest. He's still recovering in hospital, and doctors report he is lucky to still be alive. Most of those injured in the violent scuffles discharged themselves in time to catch some of the game, and the Foreign Office reports that none are in a life threatening condition. Although some fans returning home have described
15 the atmosphere as tense, football chiefs have declared these attacks to be isolated and not a true reflection of the generally good atmosphere around the stadium. After the match, Police reported that the vast majority of fans had been well behaved and said the clashes were small incidents that were dealt with swiftly.

Breaking Bulletins

Six football fans are recovering in a Barcelona hospital after being stabbed before England's World Cup qualifier match last night. They were all taken to hospital, with one reported to be seriously injured. Police blame the violence on high spirits and excessive alcohol consumed by
5 both sets of fans.

Pressure's now mounting on FIFA and the authorities to get tough with those involved in inciting violence.

a) How do the **opening sentences** of the reports follow the rules explored in the last section?

b) How has the *Breaking Bulletins* report **summarised** some of the information given in the *News Hour* report?

c) What **information** is given in the *News Hour* report that is **in addition to** the information given in the *Breaking Bulletins* report?

d) What do you think is the difference between the audience for *News Hour*, and the audience for *Breaking Bulletins*? Do they have different expectations? How does this affect the news reports?

Painting the picture

Televised news reports also rely on images to set the tone of a report and to convey the most important details.

The **first paragraph** of the text from *News Hour* was read by the newsreader in the studio.

The **second paragraph** was accompanied by **video images** of the trouble. These are brief, five- to ten-second clips of video footage, intended to highlight particular elements of the text.

5 If you were the director of the *News Hour* programme, what **images** would you use to accompany the second paragraph of the news report?

Try to think of **three** images that would help you to highlight particular parts of the text that would also convey the appropriate tone of the news report.

Set out your ideas as in the example below.

Text	Image
The stabbings happened in scuffles outside the stadium just minutes before kick-off.	Pictures of scuffles between rival fans – stadium in background.

 The headlines today

6 With a partner, note down the ***main facts*** you have learnt about writing a news report. One of you should then present the key information about writing news reports as the opening paragraph of a *News Hour* news report. The other should present the key points in the style of a *Breaking Bulletins* news report.

Both 'reporters' should remember to answer the questions **What? Who? When? Where?**

5.2 Putting on the style

Objectives:
- *investigating how meanings are changed when information is presented in different media*
- *investigating how texts are shaped by the technology they use*
- *exploring and using different degrees of formality in written and oral texts.*

In the last unit, we saw how the **audience** for the news affected the length of the text, the complexity of the sentences, and how much detail was included in the report.

In this unit, we will be looking more closely at how the audience for news reports affects the **style of the studio presentation**, and the **language** of the news reports.

Creating an image ...

1 The two pictures below show the presenters from two news programmes.

With a partner, create a word bank of at least ten adjectives that describe the style of each programme.

Consider carefully:

- **The studio set** – what impression does it give? How does it convey this impression? Think about any symbols or logos, the style of lettering in such logos, the use of colour on the set, etc.

- **The presenters** – what can you tell by their ages, their dress, their posture, etc?

2 Feedback your ideas to the rest of the class. Which words were selected by several members of the class? Was there more agreement on adjectives to describe one particular programme?

5

Choosing the right words ◈

3 Read through the following two reports.

Breaking Bulletins

Britain could soon have 'round the clock' courts in a bid to slash street crime if the government gets its way. The Home Secretary wants to punish anti-social behaviour quickly and effectively which may mean hearings at any hour of the day. A similar system has been hailed a 'winner' in New York battle against crime.

News Hour

Courts, which stay open through the night, could soon be introduced in England and Wales. According to plans revealed by the Home Secretary today, they will be used to tackle street crimes and drunkenness.

Good evening.

5 The Home Secretary revealed a startling shake up of the judiciary today as part of a new Law and Order Bill. The measures include Judges being given powers to try cases at nights and weekends under an ambitious government plan to speed up the criminal justice system. The idea has been cautiously welcomed by legal watchdogs who point to the successes
10 of a similar scheme in New York.

4 Now copy and complete the frames below, which compares the choice of language in the two reports.

News Hour

Language

England and Wales

... which stay open through the night ...

... to tackle street crimes and drunkenness ...

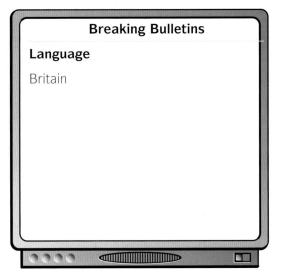

Breaking Bulletins

Language

Britain

5   What conclusions can you draw about the **formality** of the **language** used in the two reports?

6   What reasons can you suggest for these differences?

7   How does the choice of language tie up with the **presentational style** of the two news programmes? Give examples to support your opinions.

We have already discovered that televised news reports also rely on the images broadcast to set the tone of a report and to convey the most important details. This could be with video clips, or it could be with stills behind the newsreader.

8   Again working with a partner, select the particular **images/stills** you would use to accompany these news reports. Against each example, explain why you have chosen the images you have.

Set out your ideas as in the example below.

	Video images/stills	Desired effect
News Hour text		
Breaking Bulletins text		

And finally ...

9   Thinking about the key differences you have discovered between the *News Hour* news and the *Breaking Bulletins* news, write a couple of sentences summing up the style and intended audience of each news programme.

Feedback your ideas to the rest of the class and discuss why you think the different channels have tried to create such different styles.

5.3 The art of journalism

Objectives:
- *organising and presenting information, selecting appropriate material*
- *describing an event, using an appropriate degree of formality*
- *recognising how texts refer to and reflect the culture in which they were produced.*

Views of the past

1 Brainstorm words and phrases that spring to mind when you think of Britain in 1908.

2 When you have done this, see how many categories you can classify your words under, e.g. *transport, women, politics*.

3 Feedback your ideas to the rest of the class. What general conclusions can you draw about views on life in this era?

News from the past

4 Read the news report opposite. It is taken from the *Daily Mirror* in 1908, when 'suffragettes' or 'suffragists' were trying to secure democratic rights for women. (At this time, women were not allowed to vote.)

5 We have already discovered that a news report always starts by answering the questions **What? Who? When? Where?**
What answers to these questions are provided in the **opening two paragraphs** of the news report?

6 What **attitude** does the writer expect his readers to have towards the suffragettes? Which particular **words** and **phrases** reflect this attitude?

Looking back at the *Breaking Bulletins* and *News Hour* news reports on pages 73–74, we found that the *Breaking Bulletins* news report used a number of **informal** expressions, whereas *News Hour* was much more formal in its choice of language.

Suffragette on the Floor of the House of Commons

The expected demonstration in favour of women's suffrage took place last night.

Its main features were the appearance of a suffragist, Mrs Travers Symons, on the very
5 floor of the House of Commons, and the otherwise complete failure of the elaborate plans of the suffragette organisations.

The first-mentioned incident, which created a profound sensation, was due to the trustfulness
10 of Mr Idris, MP, who admitted Mrs Symons to the lobby as the daughter of an old friend, without suspecting that she intended making so startling a demonstration.

In every other direction the watchfulness of the
15 police, who were massed in overwhelming force, completely foiled the schemes of the organisers.

A deputation of suffragettes, elected at a preliminary meeting at Caxton Hall, was allowed to march under police escort nearly to the House.
20 The deputation was then informed that the Prime Minister would not consent to be interviewed.

An attempt to break through the police cordon proved unsuccessful, and the deputation, in ones and twos, were marched back to Caxton Hall under police escort. 25

Immense crowds thronged all the thoroughfares leading to Parliament Square throughout the night.

During the disturbances thirty-seven arrests were made, the prisoners including men as well 30 as women, and seven people were treated at Westminster and Charing Cross Hospitals for injuries received in the crowd.

Also, the *Breaking Bulletins* news was very brief compared with the *News Hour* version, which gave much more detail; the *Breaking Bulletins* report sometimes **summarised** information.

If *News Hour* had been around in 1908, its report on events may have read like the text below.

Use of formal language.

Summary of lengthier text in newspaper. It is more direct than newspaper.

Leading women's campaigner Mrs Travers Symons last night gained entry to the House of Commons after deceiving family friend Mr T Idris, MP. She was quickly arrested and carried out shouting by an attendant.

Shows attitude of the media towards the actions of the campaigners.

Otherwise, the plans of the campaigners were admirably thwarted by the alertness of the police, who had gathered in great force.

The suffragettes had been allowed to march almost to the House of Commons under police escort. Once there, however, their demands to meet with the Prime Minister were refused. This led to an attempt to break through the police cordon, and police had to make thirty-seven arrests.

Last paragraph – relatively simple sentence structure.

 7 Now, using your knowledge of its style of reporting, write a mock *Breaking Bulletins* news report about the suffragette's demonstration.

> **REMEMBER:**
> * *The language that you use will be less formal than the News Hour report. For instance, what phrase could you think of to replace 'leading women's campaigner?'*
> * *The report is likely to be shorter. How could you **summarise** some of the details?*
> * *Maintain the **attitude** to the event that was assumed by the media in 1908.*

8 Now, using the *News Hour* news report as a model, annotate around your *Breaking Bulletins* report, explaining the language choices you have made.

The power of words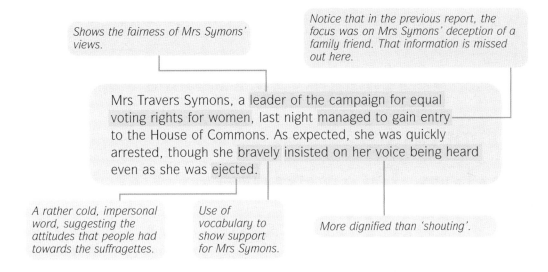

Obviously, today we find it surprising that women were not afforded the same democratic rights as men. If *News Hour* reported the incident now, then the expected attitude of the audience would be very different. For instance, the opening paragraph of the report might read:

Shows the fairness of Mrs Symons' views.

Notice that in the previous report, the focus was on Mrs Symons' deception of a family friend. That information is missed out here.

Mrs Travers Symons, a leader of the campaign for equal voting rights for women, last night managed to gain entry to the House of Commons. As expected, she was quickly arrested, though she bravely insisted on her voice being heard even as she was ejected.

A rather cold, impersonal word, suggesting the attitudes that people had towards the suffragettes.

Use of vocabulary to show support for Mrs Symons.

More dignified than 'shouting'.

The words … *she was carried out shouting by an attendant* from the original report suggest that the writer **disapproves** of Mrs Symons' actions. However, the phrase … *she bravely insisted on her voice being heard* from the mock *News Hour* report clearly indicates **support** for her actions.

9 In groups, find two more phrases in the mock *News Hour* report which show **support** for Mrs Symons, and two more phrases from the original report which show **disapproval**.

10 Now write the rest of the mock *News Hour* report on the incident. Remember, this time you should use language to show the media's **support** for the actions of Mrs Symons and the suffragettes.

News through the ages

11 What similarities, and what differences can you find when comparing news reports from 1908 with modern news reports? List three similarities, and three differences.

Reading assignment

This test is 40 minutes long

- *You should spend the first 5–10 minutes reading the text and questions carefully before you start writing your answers.*
- *Looking at the marks for each question helps you to judge how much to write for each answer.*

The passage below is taken from the *News of the World* in February 1913.

SUFFRAGIST OUTRAGES

Wanton Destruction Of Ten Courses

Famous Greens Destroyed By Women

Pursuing their campaign of reckless destruction of property, suffragists, late on Friday night or in the early hours of yesterday, did a vast amount of damage on golf courses, the most
5 serious being on the world-famous greens of the Mid-Surrey Club at Richmond.

The raid upon the club appears to have been taken part in by a considerable number of women, judging by the thoroughness of the
10 work of destruction and the wide area covered. Under the cover of a fog, suffragists attacked five greens on the men's course and four on the ladies and when the damage was discovered these greens had the appearance of miniature
15 ploughed fields instead of their customary carpet-like surface. The turf had apparently been turned up with gardeners' trowels, and on the last green on the principal course a sharp instrument had been used to cut out the words
20 'Votes For Women', while to the flag was fastened, by means of a hairpin, a piece of paper bearing a similar inscription.

The damage is very considerable, and it will be some time before the greens can be restored to their former state of excellence, but play will 25 be possible by cutting new holes on the corners of the damaged greens. Damage was also done to four of the greens on the famous championship course of the Royal St George's Club at Sandwich. Holes were scooped out as 30 though with a trowel, and papers inserted bearing the words 'Votes For Women', while damage had also been done with vitriol, with which the words 'Votes For Women' had been burned into the turf. The empty acid bottles 35 were found near the greens. The club had one stroke of luck, however. In their zeal, the women missed the new green at the seventeenth hole, and devoted their attention to the old and now little used one. 40

At the Acton course, the suffragists also pursued their stupid and outrageous campaign, digging up three or four of the best greens, and, with some acid, burning into the turf the war-cry of 'Votes For Women'. The damage is 45 estimated at £150.

1 When had the damage been done to the greens?

[1 mark]

2 What actual damage had been caused by the women?

[2 marks]

3 Why was it thought that many women had been involved in the raid on the Mid-Surrey Club?

[1 mark]

4 With what did the author compare the damage to the greens?

[1 mark]

5 What impression do you think the headlines for this article were meant to make? How do they do this?

[3 marks]

6 What had been used to damage the turf on the greens?

[1 mark]

7 What words and phrases reveal the attitude of the writer towards the suffragists?

[3 marks]

8 Why do you think the women chose famous golf courses as targets for their campaign?

[3 marks]

9 At the end of the article the journalist writes, 'At the Acton course, the suffragists also pursued their stupid and outrageous campaign, digging up three or four of the best greens, and, with some acid, burning into the turf the war-cry of "Votes For Women"'. What differences do you think might there be in a report of this type if it happened today?
You should write about:
- equal rights
- fairness of reporting
- provision of background information for readers.

[5 marks]

A6 Persuasive and argumentative writing

In this unit, you will be developing your own skills of persuasive and argumentative writing. You will trace the development of themes and ideas in texts from different eras and learn how to recognise bias and objectivity, distinguishing facts from opinions, particularly in articles concerning capital punishment. You will then go on to write your own piece of discursive writing about capital punishment.

6.1 An age-old argument

Objectives:
- *tracing the development of themes and ideas in texts*
- *recognising bias and objectivity, distinguishing facts from opinions*
- *identifying how implied meanings are conveyed in texts.*

Voicing opinions

1   With a partner, brainstorm all the reasons some people think capital punishment should be brought back in Britain.

2   Now put a number 1 next to what you consider to be the most effective argument, a number 2 against the next and so on.

3   Share your ideas with the rest of the class. Which arguments feature as the strongest within the class?

The case for ...

4   Read the article opposite. It was published on 13th July 1955 in the *Daily Mirror*. This was the day Ruth Ellis was hanged for the murder of her former lover. She was the last woman to be hanged in Britain. In the article, the writer is making a plea for the abolition of the death sentence.

CASSANDRA talks to YOU about –

THE WOMAN WHO HANGS THIS MORNING

It's a fine day for haymaking. A fine day for fishing. A fine day for lolling in the sunshine.
5 And if you feel that way – and I mourn to say that millions of you do – it's a fine day for a hanging.

If you read this before
10 **nine o'clock this morning**, the last dreadful and obscene preparations for hanging Ruth Ellis will be moving up to their fierce
15 and sickening climax. The public hangman and his assistant will have been slipped into the prison at about four o'clock
20 yesterday afternoon.

There, from what is grotesquely called 'some vantage point' and unobserved by Ruth Ellis,
25 **they will have spied upon her when she was at exercise 'to form an impression of the physique of the prisoner.'**

30 A bag of sand will have been filled to the same weight as the condemned woman and it will have been left hanging overnight
35 to stretch the rope.

Our Guilt

If you read this at nine o'clock then – short of a miracle – you and I and
40 every man and woman in the land with head to think and heart to feel will, in full responsibility, blot this woman out.

45 The hands that place the white hood over her head will not be our hands. But the guilt – and guilt there is in all this abominable
50 business – will belong to us as much as to the wretched executioner paid and trained to do the job in accordance with the
55 savage public will.

If you read this after nine o'clock, the murderess, Ruth Ellis, will have gone.

The one thing that
60 **brings stature and dignity to mankind and raises us above the beasts of the field will have been denied her –**
65 **pity and the hope of ultimate redemption.**

The medical officer will go to the pit under the trap door to see that life is

70 extinct. Then, in the barbarous wickedness of this ceremony, rejected by nearly all civilised peoples, the body will be
75 left to hang for one hour.

Dregs of Shame

If you read these words of mine at mid-day, the grave will have been dug while
80 there are no prisoners around and the Chaplain will have read the burial service after he and all of us have come so freshly from
85 disobeying the Sixth Commandment which says thou shalt not kill.

The secrecy of it all shows that if compassion is not in
90 us, then at least we still retain the dregs of shame. The medieval notice of execution will have been posted on the prison gates
95 and the usual squalid handful of louts and rubbernecks who attend these legalised killings will have had their own private
100 obscene delights.

Two Royal Commissions have protested against these horrible events. Every Home Secretary in [105] recent years has testified to the agonies of his task, and the revulsion he has felt towards his duty. None has ever claimed [110] that executions prevent murder.

Yet they go on and still Parliament has neither the resolve, nor the conviction, [115] nor the wit, nor the decency to put an end to these atrocious affairs.

When I write about capital punishment, as I have [120] often done, I get some praise and usually more abuse. In this case I have been reviled as being '*a sucker for a pretty face.*'

[125] Well, I am a sucker for a pretty face. And I am a sucker for all human faces because I hope I am a sucker for all humanity, [130] good or bad. But I prefer the face not to be lolling because of a judicially broken neck.

Yes, it is a fine day.

[135] **Oscar Wilde, when he was in Reading Gaol, spoke with melancholy of 'that little tent of blue which prisoners call [140] the sky.'**

THE TENT OF BLUE SHOULD BE DARK AND SAD AT THE THING WE HAVE DONE THIS DAY.

5   Now answer the following questions:
   a) What is the effect of the author's use of sub-headings in the article?
   b) Why are particular phrases and paragraphs in bold print?
   c) Why does the author use block capitals at the end of the piece of writing?

In persuasive writing, an author's choice of language is particularly important in putting across his/her point of view. For instance, in this article, the author uses several **emotive phrases** such as *obscene preparations* to indicate the revulsion that she feels towards the execution of Ruth Ellis.

6   Now find at least five more examples of emotive language that the author uses to display her feelings on the hanging. With each example, explain what the author is really trying to say.

7   The author of this article also frequently uses **repetition** in order to emphasise particular points. Skim-read the passage and find examples of repetition. In each case, explain the effect of the repetition.

   You should write up your findings in the form of a table, as in the following example.

Repetition	Effect of repetition
It's a fine day for haymaking. A fine day for fishing. A fine day for lolling in the sunshine.	The author repeats 'a fine day', giving three examples of pleasant traditional pursuits of a British summer. Also, she uses the word 'fine' with irony, because she considers the execution of Ruth Ellis to be anything but 'fine'.

Much of the article is written in the future tense, e.g. … *the last dreadful and obscene preparations for hanging Ruth Ellis will be moving up.*

8   Why is this more effective than waiting until the day after the execution and writing in the past tense?

9   Now look at the paragraphs that are written in the present and the past tense. What is the difference in the **content** of these paragraphs from those written in the future tense?

When considering persuasive writing, it is important to distinguish between what facts are given, and what opinions are put forward in the article.

WS 10   Complete a chart like the one started below, showing what **facts** about capital punishment are contained in the article, and where the author offers **opinions**.

Try to complete the table in your own words as far as possible.

Fact	Opinion
Public hangman enters prison at four o'clock on the day before the execution to observe condemned woman.	The guilt of execution must be shared by the British public as a whole, rather than by the hangman alone.

To sum up ...

11 With a partner, make a list of all the features you have observed in the persuasive writing of this passage.

12 Share your ideas with the rest of the class and draw up a provisional list of key points to remember when writing in this style.

6.2 A modern debate

Objectives:

- *tracing the development of themes and ideas in texts*
- *recognising bias and objectivity, distinguishing facts from opinions*
- *identifying how implied meanings are conveyed in texts*
- *using writing for thinking and learning, recording ideas as they develop.*

Voicing opinions 2

1 With a partner, brainstorm all the reasons some people think capital punishment should **not** be brought back in Britain.

2 Now put a number 1 next to what you consider to be the most effective argument, a number 2 against the next, and so on.

3 Share your ideas with the rest of the class. Which arguments feature as the strongest within the class?

4 Compare these with those drawn up in your previous lesson. Which arguments do you think are most effective – the ones for or against capital punishment?

The case against

The second article comes from the *Daily Mail*, published on 12th June 2001, the day after Timothy McVeigh was executed in America for the Oklahoma bombings.

5 Now read through the *Daily Mail* article. In this article, the writer is appealing for the restoration of the death penalty in Britain.

As Oklahoma bomber Timothy Mc Veigh is executed

Why I, as a Socialist, believe that if Mr Blair really cared about the poor he would agree to bring back 5 the rope.

No one expects Tony Blair to seek to reinstate capital punishment during the lifetime of the next 10 Parliament. But I should like him to. I am a socialist, yet as a socialist I believe the case for restoring capital punishment in Britain to be 15 overwhelming, and the opposition to it by many on the 'Left' to be illogical.

Opponents of the death penalty argue that it is 20 wrong for the state to take life. This is the line that Mr Blair takes. Yet, to be consistent, holders of this view would also have to be 25 against the state taking life in times of war. It is interesting in this context to think back to the 1999 war against Yugoslavia. 30 Then, by and large, the most enthusiastic supporters of the Nato bombing campaign on Belgrade were those

35 politicians (such as Tony Blair and Robin Cook) who are fierce in their opposition to any reintroduction of the death penalty in Britain. 40 It's a strange morality that justifies the killing of innocent make-up girls and cleaners in a Yugoslav TV studio, but not of convicted 45 serial killers at home.

The case for the death penalty rests on two tenets: first, that only convicted murderers should pay with 50 their lives; and second, that it deters. As for the first point, crucial to the maintenance of any criminal justice system is that justice 55 should be seen to be done. But in an age when convicted murderers such as Jeremy Bamber can have their own websites, it is of 60 little surprise that public confidence in the whole penal system has broken down. The second point, that capital punishment acts 65 as a deterrent, has always been disputed by the anti brigade. Yet, every country that has abolished the death

penalty has, within five 70 years, seen a dramatic increase in its murder rate. The most notable recent example of this is South Africa, with Johannesburg 75 being transformed into one of the most dangerous cities in the world.

The main reason is simple. In the days of the death 80 penalty, criminal gangs would take great care to avoid the risk of violence because they knew that, if a killing ensued, they might 85 pay with their lives.

Moreover, there is one crime for which the death penalty is arguably the only deterrent – the smuggling of 90 hard drugs. With the potential rewards running into millions of pounds, and the chances of being caught and punished slim, it is no

95 wonder that, despite 'Drug Czars' and other costly government initiatives, Britain is, in the words of the National Crime Intelligence 100 Service, 'awash with drugs'.

Compare the position with that of Singapore, a country at which liberals love to sneer. All those arriving 105 at Singapore airport are warned that anyone convicted of carrying more than a small amount of controlled drugs faces the 110 mandatory death sentence. The message could not be plainer. The result is that Singapore is one of the most drug free nations on 115 earth, and consequently one of the safest.

Even if we agree that the death penalty acts as a deterrent, what about the 120 miscarriages of justice which the anti-hanging liberals love to keep reminding us of? Inevitably, miscarriages of justice did occur when 125 Britain had the death penalty, but their number was tiny and must be set against the considerably larger number of people 130 saved from violent death by the much lower homicide rate. Now, though, there is the breakthrough of DNA testing, which narrows the 135 odds of wrong conviction to one million to one.

In the year the death penalty was abolished, (1965) there were 57 murder convictions 140 in Britain; in 1999, there were 241. We have the highest murder rate in Europe.

It is time for the people of Britain – the majority of 145 whom never wanted the death penalty abolished in the first place – to call time on this disastrous penal experiment.

150 Tony Blair claims to have made New Labour a listening party. He also claims to be 'tough on crime'. Only by bringing 155 back the ultimate deterrent can we start to take these claims seriously, and make our never deadlier streets safe once again.

6 Obviously, the author's view here is the opposite of the one expressed by 'Cassandra' in the 1955 article about Ruth Ellis. There are some ways in which the style of the writing is similar, and some ways in which it is different. Brainstorm these with a partner and then share ideas to create a whole-class spider diagram.

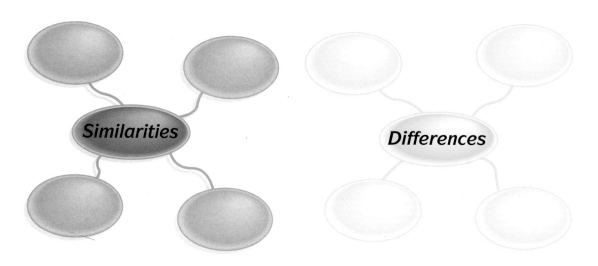

Similarities

Differences

7 Quite frequently, the journalist, Neil Clark, puts forward an opinion that is commonly held by those who are against capital punishment, and then proceeds to explain why he disagrees. For instance:

Opposing opinion	Neil Clark's opinion
Opponents of the death sentence argue that it is simply wrong to take human life.	These same opponents see Roma and Liverpool fans – innocent human life in war.

Now find further examples where the author has expressed a view that is opposite to his own, and has then argued against the view.

You may already have noticed that the author often begins a paragraph with a **topic sentence**. This is a sentence that expresses the **key point** of a paragraph. The rest of the paragraph supports the main idea by providing **supporting detail**.

For instance:

Main idea

The case for the death penalty rests on two tenets: first, that only convicted murderers should pay with their lives; and second, that it deters.

Supporting detail

Jeremy Bamber, a convicted murderer, even has his own website (*suggests current system is not a punishment*).

Supporting detail

Every country that has abolished the death penalty has, within five years, seen a dramatic increase in its murder rate.

 8 Now find more examples of this technique being used in the text, and complete your own diagrams like the one above to show the relationship between the 'main idea' and the 'supporting details' (Note: in this example, there are **two** supporting details. However, a main idea may be supported by **any number** of supporting details – even one!)

Closing comments

It could be said that the article about Ruth Ellis sought to **persuade** the reader that capital punishment was wrong, whereas the article published after the execution of the Oklahoma bomber set out to **argue** the case for bringing back capital punishment.

9 In a group, prepare a brief statement of no more than twenty-five words on the key differences between **persuasive** writing and **argumentative** writing. Read it to the rest of the class.

6.3 Putting a case together

Objectives:

- *investigating the different ways familiar ideas are explored and presented by different writers*
- *analysing the overall structure of a text to identify how key ideas are developed*
- *extending a range of connectives to 'signpost' an argument.*

Emphasising the point

1 When arguing a point of view, a writer has to find many different ways of saying **right** or **wrong**, **good** or **bad**.

a) Using a thesaurus, make a word bank of alternatives for these words.

b) Which of the words you have found do you think will be most effective at making a point?

The building tools

There are a number of words and phrases that you can use when constructing an argument that help to **signpost** your work.

Yet, *to be consistent* ... *The case for* ... *As for the first point* ... *Moreover* ... *Even if* *we agree* ... *Only by* ...

Below are some other words and phrases that are useful in argumentative writing because they help you to compare views:
however, alternatively, despite this, on the other hand, equally, nevertheless, whereas

Writers also need key phrases to support their views with examples and illustration such as:

for example	*for instance*	*such as*
as revealed by	*to show that*	*as indicated by*

2 Look back over this unit as a whole. Make an advice list for a partner, in which you suggest 'ten top tips' that will help him/her to put together a good piece of argumentative writing.

Successful or not?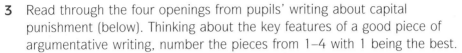

3 Read through the four openings from pupils' writing about capital punishment (below). Thinking about the key features of a good piece of argumentative writing, number the pieces from 1–4 with 1 being the best.

Some people argue that we should never lawfully be able to take human life, as this only takes us down to the level of the criminal. However, I believe that some people commit such dreadful crimes that they deserve to lose their own lives. Take the case of Fred and Rose West, who were found guilty of a series of morbid murders. Surely, their crimes were so extreme, and the proof of them so complete, it seems to me to be totally justifiable that they should pay with their own lives.

I don't think capital punishment is a good idea, but on the other hand, in some ways it is. It isn't because people should not kill anybody, even murderers. It is because look what happened to Timothy McVeigh, the Oklahoma bomber, who was executed. That was a good idea, I think. On the other hand, will it bring anybody back? Another example is the Ruth Ellis case, when she was convicted of murder in 1955.

The Bulger case is one that has been on the news recently. Jamie Bulger was killed and his killers, who were only ten years old, were detained for eight years. They were recently granted a release, but they have not yet been freed as there are threats against them. I know that what they did was dreadful, but in their case, I don't think it would be fair to condemn them to death.

I am very much against the reintroduction of capital punishment, as I do not believe that it would serve any purpose in a modern society. It could be argued that criminals will avoid using violence because they fear the possibility of themselves being executed. However, one only has to look at the frightening example of the USA, where violent crime is far more frequent than it is in Britain, despite a penal system which includes the death sentence.

4 Having placed the four openings on a scale from 'best' to 'worst', now take each opening in turn and explain what you believe to be the **strengths** and **weaknesses** of each.

5 Now write a target for each student, suggesting ways in which they could improve their writing.

A battle of skills

6 Working with a partner, take either the **for capital punishment** or the **against capital punishment** viewpoint and take it in turns to make a statement supporting your point of view. You should try to include the 'signposting' words in your statements. The first one to hesitate loses.

6.4 Putting the case

Objectives:
- *organising and presenting information selecting appropriate material*
- *presenting a case persuasively, making selective use of evidence*
- *developing and signposting arguments to make the logic clear to the reader.*

Collecting the final evidence

1 Note down the main arguments for and against capital punishment you have discovered in this unit.

2 Highlight the ones you think are most effective.

Defence or prosecution?

3 Now write your response to the question:

Do you believe that capital punishment should be reintroduced in Britain?

A

First, you should state clearly your own point of view:

On balance, I am in favour of capital punishment.

I do not believe that it would be right to reintroduce capital punishment.

B

Continue your essay by putting forward a view that is opposite to your own. This gives you a chance to answer that opinion later on.

Some people argue that no human being should ever have the right to take the life of another human being – even a murderer.

The 'bring back the rope' brigade seem to believe that its reintroduction would cut crime at a stroke, simply out of fear of the death penalty.

C

Then go on to put forward the view that you hold. Don't forget to use your signpost words and phrases.

However, I believe that there is much to be said for the old biblical notion of 'an eye for an eye'. Put simply, occasionally the taking of human life is justifiable.

For all that, I'm afraid that I see little evidence of this in countries that have capital punishment as part of their penal system.

D

Next, give evidence to support your view. Again, use your signpost words and phrases to help you to structure your writing.

For instance, to take the case of Oklahoma bomber Timothy Mc Veigh, he took the lives of 168 men, women and children, and never even expressed any remorse for his crime. Surely, here is a clear example of how execution is sometimes justifiable.

In the United States of America, for example, has the maintenance of capital punishment led to crime – free streets? It certainly has not. In fact, the United States boasts one of the highest crime rates in the world.

E

Finally, briefly state your own view again, picking out the major pieces of evidence that support this view.

In conclusion, then, I believe that capital punishment should be reintroduced.

The evidence that capital punishment is a deterrent outweighs the idea that ...

Repeat the process, going through the cycle B–E as you progress through your essay.

The jury's out

When you have completed your first draft, swap with a partner. Ask them to highlight in one colour all the really effective points and in another colour, the points that need expanding or putting more forcefully. Bear these points in mind when redrafting.

Reading assignment

This test is 40 minutes long

- *You should spend the first 5–10 minutes reading the text and questions carefully before you start writing your answers.*
- *Looking at the marks for each question helps you to judge how much to write for each answer.*

The article below was written by the Voluntary Euthanasia Society.

What is the VES?

The Voluntary Euthanasia Society aims to make it legal for a terminally ill adult, who is suffering unbearably to be allowed to request medical assistance to die if that's what they want. We are a not-for-profit organisation which campaigns strictly within the law, to change it. All our funds come from
5   our members – ordinary individuals who believe in CHOICE.

Opinion polls show that over 80% of the British public agree with changing the law. Evidence shows that terminally ill people are already helped to die each day in Britain, behind closed doors. A new law must provide everyone with choices at the end of life. It must also ensure that
10 where people are helped to die, there are transparent legal processes to protect vulnerable patients.

Everyone wants 'a good death' – the literal meaning of the Greek word 'euthanasia'. Most of us will die suddenly and painlessly, and won't need to ask for the help of the medical profession. Palliative care and hospices
15 are able to relieve the pain of many terminal illnesses. However, many of us have seen friends and relatives die long drawn-out deaths and thought, 'In their shoes I would like to have a choice about how and when I die'.

The law must be changed for people who have exhausted all medical alternatives and made an informed and personal decision that they have
20 had enough. We all have a basic human right to 'a good death'.

What is voluntary euthanasia?
Voluntary euthanasia has come to mean a doctor deliberately ending someone's life at that person's request, in order to relieve intractable suffering. This is against the law in the UK, and any doctor who helps a
25 terminally ill patient to die is open to a charge of murder. The Voluntary Euthanasia Society campaigns to change the law, so that terminally ill adults can legally request medical help to die at a time and in a manner of their own choosing.

How can we protect against abuse?
30 The Netherlands and Oregon have laws which work well in allowing choice at the end of life and protecting vulnerable people. Why can't we have the same here?

When assisted dying becomes a legal choice in Britain, it is equally important that strict safeguards are included in any law.

35 For example:

- Getting at least two doctors (one of these must be a consultant) to establish that the adult patient is suffering unbearably from a terminal illness, and that the patient's request is wholly voluntary.
- If either doctor suspects the patient is suffering from a mental disorder
40 (such as depression), the patient should be referred for psychiatric evaluation.
- The patient must be advised about all the treatment and care alternatives, in particular palliative care.
- The patient's request must be deemed to be free from coercion by a
45 court of law.
- No person in the process may derive financial benefit from the patient's death.
- There must be a waiting period of at least a week between the patient making the request and the doctor helping them to die.

1 According to the article what is the exact meaning of the word 'euthanasia'?

[1 mark]

2 Why is the word CHOICE written in capitals in the article?

[1 mark]

3 When do most people first start thinking about euthanasia according to the article?

[1 mark]

4 Which countries/states have already legalised euthanasia according to the article?

[1 mark]

5 What effect do you think the phrases 'not-for-profit' and 'strictly within the law' (lines 3-4) are intended to have on the reader?

[2 marks]

6 Explain the meaning of the following words and phrases, as they are used in the passage:
transparent legal processes (line 10)   *terminally ill* (line 25)
vulnerable people (line 31)

[3 marks]

7 What kind of evidence does the article use to make its point?

[2 marks]

8 What emotive words and phrases are used to describe people's situations to make us feel as if the present situation is wrong?

[2 marks]

9 What is the effect of the sub-headings in this article?

[2 marks]

10 How does the article both inform and persuade the reader?
You should write about:
- the layout of the article
- the language used in the article
- the actual content of the article.

[5 marks]

In this unit, you will be exploring poetry from different times and cultures, based on the theme 'My Background'. You will learn how poets represent their viewpoints, their ideas and their cultural identities through their poetry, and examine the images they use to achieve this. You will then use this understanding to write your own poetry.

7.1 Painting pictures with words

Objectives:
- *investigating the different ways in which writers explore and present familiar themes*
- *identifying the ways in which meaning is conveyed in texts*
- *recognising how texts reflect the culture in which they were produced.*

Collecting memories

1 Think back to your very first school and your first teacher. Now brainstorm words and phrases that could describe your memories, e.g. *large, green pencil sharpener*, *colourful wall displays*, *magical stories*.

2 Now share your memories with the rest of the class. What similarities are there in the memories? Keep your brainstormed notes for later use.

Images from the past

3 Now read the poem 'In Mrs Tilscher's Class' by Carol Ann Duffy. In this poem, the poet is reminiscing about her primary school when she was in the class of a teacher called Mrs Tilscher. As you read the poem, see how many of your memories are similar to the ones in the poem.

4 Now study the poem more closely, looking carefully at the adjectives the poet has used to create different moods. Which words and phrases do you think are particularly effective at creating the image of early school days? Why?

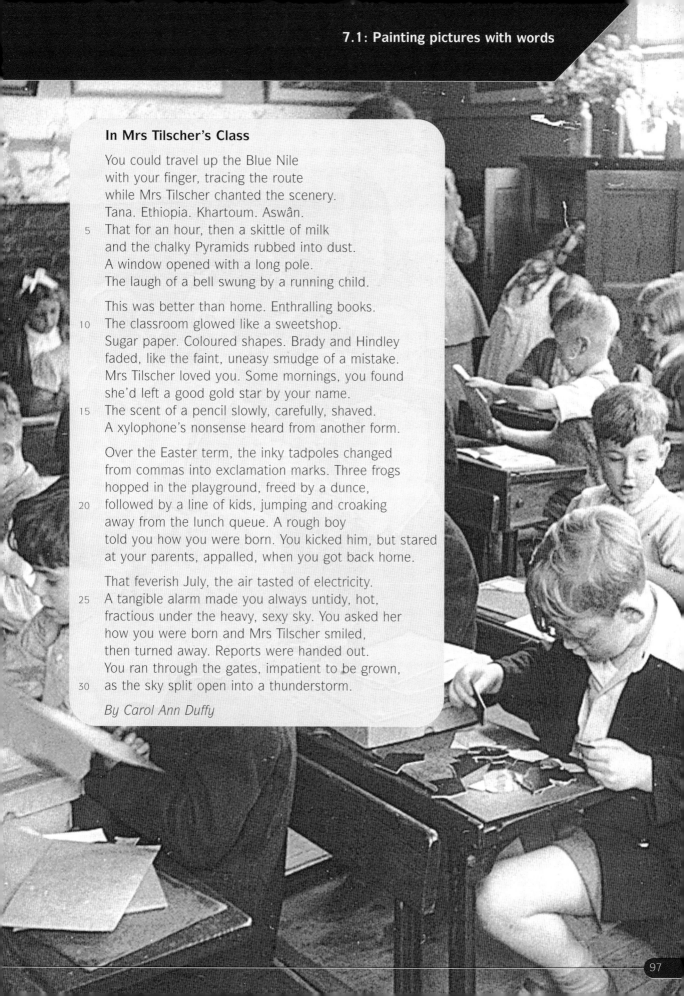

In Mrs Tilscher's Class

You could travel up the Blue Nile
with your finger, tracing the route
while Mrs Tilscher chanted the scenery.
Tana. Ethiopia. Khartoum. Aswân.
5   That for an hour, then a skittle of milk
and the chalky Pyramids rubbed into dust.
A window opened with a long pole.
The laugh of a bell swung by a running child.

This was better than home. Enthralling books.
10 The classroom glowed like a sweetshop.
Sugar paper. Coloured shapes. Brady and Hindley
faded, like the faint, uneasy smudge of a mistake.
Mrs Tilscher loved you. Some mornings, you found
she'd left a good gold star by your name.
15 The scent of a pencil slowly, carefully, shaved.
A xylophone's nonsense heard from another form.

Over the Easter term, the inky tadpoles changed
from commas into exclamation marks. Three frogs
hopped in the playground, freed by a dunce,
20 followed by a line of kids, jumping and croaking
away from the lunch queue. A rough boy
told you how you were born. You kicked him, but stared
at your parents, appalled, when you got back home.

That feverish July, the air tasted of electricity.
25 A tangible alarm made you always untidy, hot,
fractious under the heavy, sexy sky. You asked her
how you were born and Mrs Tilscher smiled,
then turned away. Reports were handed out.
You ran through the gates, impatient to be grown,
30 as the sky split open into a thunderstorm.

By Carol Ann Duffy

When a poet wants to create a vivid, visual picture in the reader's mind, they often use **imagery** which uses comparison to 'paint the picture.'

> **Imagery** can be sub-divided into three categories:
>
> **Similes** – which compare using the words like or as, e.g. *He ran like the wind*.
>
> **Metaphors** – which compare but without using the words *like* or *as* so they seem more powerful and real, e.g. *The sun was a ball of fire*.
>
> **Personification** – where an object or feeling is described as having human qualities, e.g. *The door sighed*.

5   Now look back at 'In Mrs Tilscher's Class' and find examples of these different types of imagery. When you have found them, experiment with writing them in different ways that could change the mood of the poem.

6   Read and discuss the poem below. Grace Nichols, from Guyana, is also writing about her past. She conveys the idea that that the food she used to eat as a child is an image that represents her culture and the warmth of her early life.

This is set against an image of '*cold*' London, perhaps suggesting her feelings about the mood of the city as well as being true with regard to the weather.

Like a Beacon

In London
every now and then
I get this craving
for *my mother's food*
5   I leave art galleries
in search of *plantains
saltfish / sweet potatoes*

I need this link

I need this touch
10   of home
swinging my bag
like a beacon
against *the cold*

By Grace Nichols

7   Now, brainstorm words that could replace the text in italics to reflect the viewpoints of different people or cultures. Try to think of groups of words that conjure up images of different groups of people. (It doesn't have to be about food!) How many different versions can you create?

A poet's use of language (ws)

8 In the poem below, some of the text has been removed. In each case, four options have been written below the poem. Decide which phrase you think was used in the **original** poem. Note down the phrase of your choice, and write a sentence or two explaining the reasons for your choice. You should complete this activity as shown in the framework at the bottom of the page.

Immigrant

November '63: eight months in London.
I pause on the low bridge to watch the pelicans:
they float swanlike, arching their white necks
over only slightly ruffled bundles of wings,
5 burying awkward beaks in the lake's water.

I clench _____**(A)**_____ in my Marks and Spencer's jacket
and _____**(B)**_____ my accent _____**(C)**_____:
St James's Park; St James's Park; St James's Park.

By Fleur Adcock

Phrases		
A	**B**	**C**
my hands	quietly try out	to see what it is like
large fingers	happily attempt	once again
cold fists	confidently attempt	for the first time
my fists	secretly test	to my friend

(A) I think the phrase should be '_____'

because the word '_____' shows ....

and the word '_____' suggests..

....

(B) I think the phrase should be '_____'

because...

....

(C) I think the phrase should be '_____'

because...

....

Getting the picture

9 With a partner, prepare a quick tips guide for a new poet, in which you explain what **imagery** is and how this affects the language you choose to use.

7.2 The best words in the best order

Objectives:
- *investigating the different ways in which writers explore and present familiar themes*
- *identifying the ways in which meaning is conveyed in texts*
- *analysing the overall structure of a text to identify how key ideas are developed.*

Word sounds – word association

1 Brainstorm fifteen words that you associate with love, and fifteen that you associate with violence. Note down your ideas in two columns, as has been started for you below:

Love	Violence
joy	stab
happiness	rip
caress	smash
cuddle	hate

When you have this, read the words aloud, and then consider the following questions:

a) What is the main difference in the **sounds** of the two columns of words?

b) What brings about this difference in sounds? (You should you think about individual letters and letter sounds when answering this question. Comment on use of consonants and use of vowels.)

The language of poetry

Opposite is a poem called 'I Remember', by Thomas Hood. In the poem, the poet is looking back to his childhood, and comparing his feelings then with his feelings as an adult.

2 Eight words have been deleted from the poem, and they have been placed in the box below. Try to replace them correctly, listening carefully to the sound of the poem as you read through it.

I Remember, I Remember

I remember, I remember,
   The house where I was born,
The little window where the _____
   Came peeping in at morn;
5 He never came a wink too soon
   Nor brought too long a day,
But now, I often wish the night
   Had borne my breath away.

I remember, I remember,
10   The roses, red and white;
The _____, and the lily-cups
   Those flowers made of _____!
The lilacs where the robin built,
   And where my brother set
15 The laburnum on his birthday,
   The tree is living yet!

I remember, I remember,
   Where I was used to swing;
And thought the air must rush as _____
20   To swallows on the wing:
My spirit _____ in feathers then,
   That is so _____ now,
The _____ pools could hardly cool
   The fever on my brow!

25 I remember, I remember,
   The fir trees dark and high;
I used to think their slender tops
   Were close against the sky:
It was a childish ignorance,
30   But now 'tis little joy
To know I'm farther off from _____
   Than when I was a boy.

By Thomas Hood

The missing words			
heavy	*flew*	*summer*	*Heaven*
fresh	*sun*	*violets*	*light*

3   Now answer the questions below to help you to understand how writers use **language** and **imagery** to express their views.

   a) Explain how the poet uses colourful images in order to reflect upon his childhood.

   b) What do the lines: *And thought the air must rush as fresh* / *To swallows on the wing* tell the reader about the poet's feelings about his early life?

   c) How does the poet use language to show the contrast in his spirits between childhood and adulthood?

   d) What do you think the poet is trying to say in the last three lines of the poem?

4   If you wanted to use images of weather to reflect upon a depressing, sad feeling, then what sort of weather would you choose? If you wanted to suggest happiness and joy, what images would you then choose?

 5   Look back at the four poems you have studied so far in this section. Make an 'image table' by selecting five images from the poems, and explaining why you think they are effective. An example of this is shown below.

Image	Effectiveness
The classroom glowed like a sweet shop	A sweet shop is a place of fantasy and enjoyment and the colours in the classroom are like the multi-coloured desirable contents of a sweet shop. It is a very pleasant image.

Vocabulary – choosing your words carefully

6   Try preparing a deletion activity for another pupil. List about ten words that you would delete from one of the poems, and explain why you have chosen them. Now get your partner to fill in the gaps, thinking about images and sound.

The right words

7   Now go back to your list of 'love' and 'violence' words on page 100 and work each word into a longer image.

   Share your images with the rest of the class.

7.3　Poetry from your background

Objectives:

- *experimenting with figurative language*
- *experimenting with different language choices to convey meaning*
- *re-reading work to consider the effect on the reader.*

Using your senses

1　Think about a particular location. It might be your kitchen at home, the school science lab, a local park, your bedroom, a beach, a street, etc.

Write down your location. Write five phrases below it, one describing a sight, one a sound, one a smell, one a taste and one a touch. It might look like this:

The Beach

Ice cream cones
Kite snapping in the wind
Seaweed
Salt on my lips
Pebbles hard under my feet

2　Read out your sense descriptions to others in your group. They should try to guess what the location is. After the location has been guessed, talk about which parts of the 'sense descriptions' are the most effective, and why.

A true image

We have already discovered that a metaphor is where a writer writes about something as if it were really something else. It could be called an 'imaginative substitution'. For instance, the following are metaphors:

He is an ass.　　　　　　　*The biting wind.*
The tension is electric.　　*Clouds hurry across the horizon.*

They are all metaphors because none of them is **literally** true. A man can't really be an ass; wind doesn't actually bite, etc. However, they are **images** that can take the reader closer to the truth, the feeling or the emotion. For example, the phrase The biting wind is more effective than The cold wind, because it expresses the physical pain that such coldness can cause.

Look at these two lists. Which list has more dramatic potential? Why?

Leaves move	*Leaves tremble*
The moon shines	*The moon grins*
Rain falls	*Rain weeps*
Driftwood is	*Driftwood sleeps*

The second list uses **personification**. Remember, this is where inanimate objects are given human action, motivation or emotion. Personification can add considerable power because it creates dynamic pictures in the reader's mind, helping the reader to engage with, or relate to, objects.

Now you are going to use personification to develop your ideas around 'The Beach'.

3 First, think of around ten to fifteen things that you would see on a beach. The list has been started below.

deck chairs
pebbles
ice cream cones

4 Next, make a list of verbs that describe human and animal actions. Again, the list has been started below.

grumble
shout
doze
snigger

5 Now, pair up five objects with five verbs.
　　Pebbles doze　　*Ice cream cones snigger*

6 Then, use these ideas to begin shaping a brief six- to ten-line poem, as has been started in the example below.

> *Pebbles doze in the afternoon sun,*
> *Heavy, tired.*
> *An ice cream cone skitters past*
> *Stops, sniggers,*
> *Then is whisked on ...*

Sharing your response

7 When you have finished, once more read your poem to others in your group. Consider which are the most effective lines in each poem. Why? Think about:
   a) Use of the **senses**.
   b) Use of **language**.
   c) Use of **metaphor**, especially **personification**.

The best of the rest

8 Each group should select two lines from the work of the whole group that they think are particularly powerful. These can be read to the class, and the group should briefly explain why they chose this line.

7.4   Poetry in your words

Objectives:
- *experimenting with figurative language*
- *experimenting with different language choices to convey meaning*
- *re-reading work to consider the effect on the reader*
- *presenting poetry in different forms and styles.*

Poems often reflect the culture of the people that wrote them, both in their subject matter and in the language that they use. You are going to write a poem that reflects your own culture. You are going to base your poem on a **rap**, as this is something that most people are familiar with.

The language of your culture

1   First, think about your own language. Are there words that you use in a particular context, such as *wicked*, *dark* or *safe*? Take five minutes to **brainstorm** words or expressions that reflect your **culture** – your age, your ethnicity, the place where you live, etc.

2   Share your ideas with the class. Keep a word bank of the useful and important words and phrases that you might want to use.

Telling the tale

3   Next, think of a **short story** you want to tell. It could be a funny story, or a serious one. For instance:

> My story is about a pupil handing in a picture to his art teacher.
> The teacher thought it was offensive, but the pupil's dad thought it was really good.

As you can see, you only need a **brief idea** here.

4   The next thing you'll need is a **beat** or **rhythm**.

You can check the rhythm by tapping your foot.

> I handed in my picture, and my teacher said,
> 'You have strange ideas whirling in your head.
> Take it home with you, I'll write a little note.'
> 'Please come and see me' I think is what she wrote.
> I took the picture home and gave it to my dad
> He said, 'Hey this is **dark**, son, this is really **bad**.
> The colours they are **wicked**, I really like the red,
> The gooey bit trickling from your teacher's head.
> And the way you've shaped the axe is really cool
> And how the teacher's tipping forward off his stool ...'

5   The sample rap above has also included another thing you'll need to write a rap: a rhyme pattern of A-A-B-B. Notice that the last word in the first line (said) rhymes with the last word in the second line (head), and the last word in the third line (note) rhymes with the last word in the fourth line (wrote).

6   Notice also how the words that we brainstormed earlier are used in the poem, though here they are given a bit of a 'twist', because they are used by the pupil's dad.

7   Using your rhyme scheme and your planner, start to put together your rap.

Perform your poem

8   Rap is, of course, written to be performed, not merely read from the page. When you have written your rap, rehearse a performance of it with others in your group.

Some of them, or all of them, could be performed to the class as a whole.

A world of poetry

9   A rap is a particular form of poetry. However, list the skills have you been developing and practising in this unit that would be useful in considering different types of poems?

Writing assignment

Major task: you should spend about 40 minutes answering this question.

Your writing will be marked for:
- *how you structure and punctuate sentences (5 marks)*
- *how you organise paragraphs (5 marks)*
- *the overall impact of your writing on the reader (15 marks)*
- *the accuracy of your spelling (5 marks)*

A major publisher has decided to publish a selection of fantasy maps together with descriptions of these lands for children.

However, the map printed opposite has appeared on their desks without a description to go alongside it. Your task is to write the description so that the map can be included in the book.

Study the map and then, using the skills of building up an image practised in this unit, write your own description of Fantasy Island (this should be organised in paragraphs and not as a poem).

It is important to plan your ideas first before you begin to write.
Use a planning grid like the one below:

Image on map to be described	*Words and phrases to describe this*

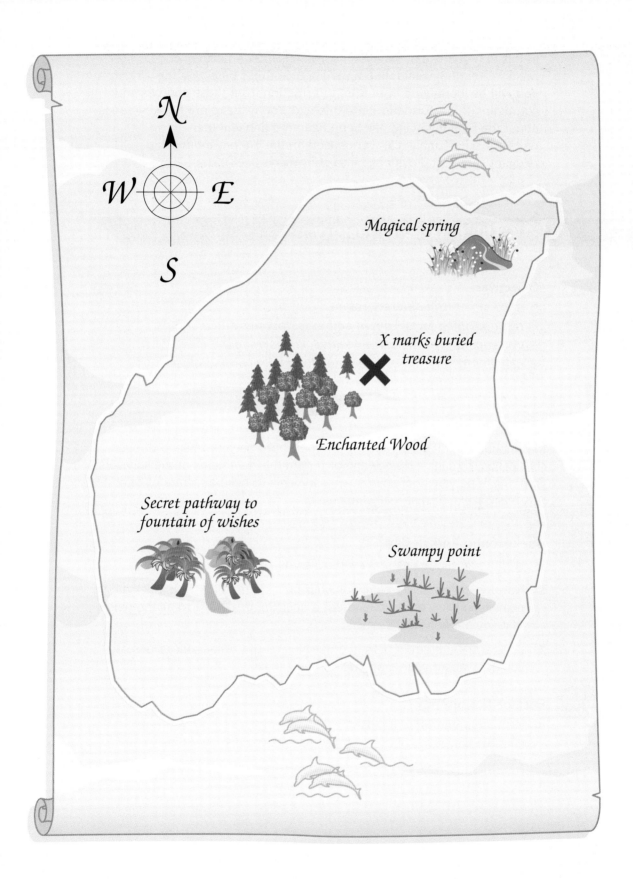

A8 In search of the truth

In this unit you will be developing your skills as an active, critical reader through investigating a variety of sources based on the *Titanic*. You will be identifying important information from these sources and combining this information into one text. You will explore how evidence about the fateful voyage has been gathered and will then go on to write a piece of analytical work based on the *Titanic*, integrating relevant supporting evidence into your work.

 ## 8.1 The making of history

Objectives:
- *making notes in different ways*
- *distinguishing facts from hypotheses, theories and opinions*
- *developing your skills as an active, critical reader*
- *using writing for thinking and learning by recording ideas.*

Tales from the past

Many stories and theories about the *Titanic* have been developed through speculation, through evidence and also from the statements of the survivors. From this wide variety of sources we can begin to build a picture of what it was really like and what really happened.

 ### Background knowledge

1 With a partner, brainstorm everything you know about the *Titanic*.

2 Now look again at the points on your brainstorm. Mark with a tick all the points you know are facts and put a question mark next to all the points that you are not sure are facts.

3 Look at the pattern of ticks and question marks. What conclusions can you draw about your knowledge of the *Titanic*?

 ### Fact or fiction? ⓦ

4 With a partner, read the extracts on pages 111–112. As you read, consider why some of these stories have developed over time.

NO BINOCULARS

The story about the *Titanic* being without any binoculars for the look-outs and crew is *almost* correct. *Titanic's* Second Officer had originally been David Blair, but when Henry Wilde was assigned to *Titanic's* maiden voyage because of his experience as Chief Officer aboard *Olympic*, the remaining officers' ranks were changed, and Blair was the one removed to make way for Wilde. The binoculars were actually aboard the vessel, inside a locker in the cabin that Blair had originally occupied between Belfast and Southampton, although it would seem that nobody knew they were there at all.

BUNKER FIRE

The story regarding a fire in one of *Titanic's* massive coal bunkers is indeed true. The fire is believed to have been burning when *Titanic* left Belfast, and it was not until two or three days later that it was finally extinguished, this being done by teams of firemen and trimmers digging out almost all of the coal to enable the seat of the fire to be doused. Some *Titanic* scholars believe that the intense heat of the fire could have led to some parts of the hull being seriously weakened, and actually assisted in the break-up and sinking of the vessel.

UNSINKABLE

Over the years *Titanic* has been described as the `Unsinkable Ship´. This came about because at the time of *Titanic's* fitting out, there was a special edition of *The Shipbuilder* magazine, in which *Titanic* was described as `practically unsinkable´, due to the double bottom, watertight compartments etc. White Star certainly never described her as such, but with the passing of time, many books and films go so far as to suggest that they did.

MORE LIFEBOATS

Many people believe that so many people died as a result of there not being enough lifeboats for everyone on the ship. But if you study exactly what happened on the night, you must appreciate that not only was time at a premium, but also that suitable manpower was totally inadequate. There were just over 50 members of the deck crew who were trained to launch a lifeboat, and the loading of the boats that night was painfully slow. Couple that with the near disaster of lowering one boat on to another, and the interference from outsiders, and you begin to understand the theory.

Finally, the proof of the above theory is this – the crew didn't even have time to hang the two collapsible lifeboats 'A' and 'B' in their respective port and starboard davits. Time had run out, and the two Englehardts had to float off the sinking ship.

MUMMY OF AMEN-RA

Titanic sank because it carried in its hold the Mummy of Amen-Ra, a mummy that carried a curse of death and destruction. Of course, this is pure fiction, although strangely, it is born out of fact. During the voyage, the famous spiritualist, William T. Stead, had told a dinner party the story of the Mummy of Amen-Ra, which was actually on display at the time at London's British Museum. In the days and weeks after the disaster, many incorrect or totally fabricated stories were published in the press, and the story of the Mummy of Amen-Ra actually being aboard the fateful liner was born.

*From **Titanic Titanic!** website ©Titanic Titanic! 1999 2000 2001*

5 Now study the extracts carefully. They contain many **facts**, some completely fabricated **stories**, and some **theories** based on **supposition** (drawing conclusions from facts we do have).

Draw up a table like the one below, showing which ideas were completely made up, and giving reasons why you think people believed these tales.

Main ideas of untrue stories about Titanic	Reasons why people might have believed them.

6 Now concentrate on the extracts that suggest **theories** about what might have happened. We sometimes refer to theories as **hypotheses**.

Draw up a second table like the one below, showing the theories that have developed over time and the evidence that has been used to support these.

Theories about Titanic	Evidence used to support them

Putting the picture together

When you read non-fiction, you often have to study various documents and texts, and bring together facts from different sources. This means that you have to act as a 'detective', making note of important information and clues, ignoring unimportant details and drawing all of these together to form a complete picture of what happened.

THE WARNINGS
Many ships had sent through ice warnings to the *Titanic* in the days before the collision. On 11th April, she received six warnings, five more on the 12th, three more on the 13th, and seven on the 14th. There was now no way that the captain or the rest of the crew would have been unaware of the dangers that lay ahead of *Titanic*.

7 Read through the ice warnings listed on page 114, considering carefully whether the crew or captain could have done more to prevent this disaster.

Ice Warnings Received by Titanic		
Date/Time	Ship	Message
14/4 9.00am	*Caronia* – Eastbound, New York to Liverpool, Queenstown. The message was delivered to the bridge, where Captain Smith posted it for his officers to read.	'Captain, *Titanic* – West-bound steamers report bergs, growlers and field ice in 42° N, from 49° to 51° W, April 12th. Compliments, Barr'
14/4 1.42pm	*Baltic* – Eastbound, New York to Liverpool, Queenstown. This message was delivered to Captain Smith as he talked to Bruce Ismay. Ismay pocketed the piece of paper, and later showed it to several passengers. At 7.15pm, Smith asked for its return, when it was finally posted in the chart room.	'Greek steamer *Athenia* reports passing icebergs and large quantities of field ice today in latitude 41° 51' N, longitude 49° 52' W. Wish you and *Titanic* all success. Commander.'
14/4 1.45pm	*Amerika* – **This message was actually a private one to the US Hydrographic Office in Washington DC, overheard by Titanic's radio operators. Regrettably, it never made its way to the bridge.**	'*Amerika* passed two large icebergs in 41° 27' N, 50° 8' W on April 14.'
14/4 7.30pm	*Californian* – This message was actually to *Antillian*, but overheard by *Titanic*'s radio operators. This was delivered by Bride to the bridge, although Captain Smith was not made aware of it. He was in the à la carte restaurant, dining with the Wideners.	'To Captain, *Antillian*: Six-thirty pm, apparent ship's time; latitude 42° 3' N, longitude 49° 9' W. Three large bergs 5 miles to the southward of us. Regards, Lord.'
14/4 9.40pm	*Mesaba* – This message never reached the bridge. Harold Bride was getting some much-needed sleep, and Jack Phillips was busy on the key sending and receiving commercial traffic to Cape Race.	'From *Mesaba* to *Titanic*. In latitude 42° N to 41° 25', longitude 49° W to longitude 50° 30' W, saw much heavy pack ice and great number large icebergs, also field ice, weather good, clear.'

Detectives' summing up

8 Using all of the information from the ice warnings chart, with a partner draw up your list of reasons why the *Titanic* did not seem to heed these warnings.

9 Now draw up a list of action points you would have given as advice to other ships at the time to ensure this kind of disaster never happened again.

10 Share your ideas with the rest of the class. Using the information studied in this section, what main conclusions could you draw about the organisation aboard the *Titanic*?

Questioning the text

11 Thinking about the work you have done in this section, what questions should we ask as readers when studying an information text? Note down your ideas with a partner and share them with the rest of the class.

8.2 Painting the past with words and pictures

Objectives:
- *undertaking independent research using a range of reading strategies*
- *combining information from various sources into one coherent document*
- *making notes in different ways*
- *using writing for thinking and learning by recording ideas.*

A different time?

1 Look at the statements below which look at the preparations for the departure of the *Titanic*. Which of these statements do you think point to a different era and which do you think would be as true today as then?

A
> A couple of firemen employed by the liner were enjoying a last-minute pint in one of Southampton's many public houses and would miss the departure.

B
> The passengers were all aboard, the majority of them on deck bidding farewell to friends and families they would not see for some time if ever again.

C
> Many people, especially in steerage, (third class) were making a one-way journey, looking for a better life in America. They had sold everything they owned and now their worldly belongings would fill just a couple of bags, or a trunk.

D

> For the wealthier people in first-class, accommodation this was merely a pleasure trip and an attempt to gain social status.

E

> New friendships and business contacts would be formed and developed which would continue the trade of the wealthy businessmen.

A snapshot of a bygone era

To have a clearer understanding of the impact of the *Titanic* disaster, we have so set it against other events at the time and ensure we understand its place in history. Many of the things that happened seem unbelievable now, but at the time they were perfectly understandable.

3   To understand this event fully, you will need to do some research of your own. First, take the events listed below, and put a date to each of them. You will need to think about how you would look these up. You could use:

- the school library
- a local library
- an encyclopaedia
- an electronic encyclopaedia
- the Internet.

> **REMEMBER:**
>
> *You are looking for particular pieces of information in this activity. Therefore, you are expected to scan the texts that you find. This means to look quickly over a text, to locate a key word or key information.*

The events

Women get the vote
The First World War begins
The Titanic *sinks*
The first radio broadcast is transmitted
The first television broadcast is transmitted
Wall Street Crash (the collapse of the American economy)
Slavery is abolished in North America
Queen Victoria dies.

4   When you have done this, record the main points of each event in a way that you will find easy to refer back to.

Presenting your information

Now think about the ways you might present your research information in sequence to make an **impact** on the reader.

In groups:

5 List the events in order, from the earliest to the latest. This ensures you know the span of years that you have to cover in your presentation.

6 Consider how you might present the information to have a **visual impact** and **convey information clearly**.

   a) How will you represent each event/time? What sort of map/diagram/illustration/graphic will you use?

   b) How will you represent different gaps in time?

   c) How will you ensure that your presentation is informative – what is the relationship between the text and illustration? Where will you place your text?

7 When you have thought through all of the points above, sketch out your presentation on a large sheet of paper. At this stage, all text/illustrations etc. should be rough, to be used as a guide and a way of checking that your ideas work in practice.

You might want to include a layout like the one below:

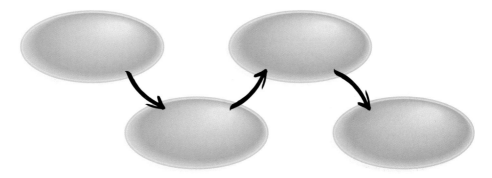

8 Make a final draft of your presentation.

Explain your designs

9 Now display your work so that others can see it.
   Explain to the class:

   a) How you decided to present your work.

   b) Why you chose this method.

   c) Which elements you think have the most impact on the reader.

   d) Which elements you would change or adapt if you had more time.

8.3 Making a case for history

Objectives:
- *organising and presenting information*
- *presenting a case persuasively, making selective use of evidence*
- *developing and signposting arguments*
- *integrating evidence into writing to support analysis.*

Sorting out …

There are many different ways in which we may like to organise information.

1 Arrange the words below into different groups. You can decide how you group them together. It is not that important **how** you group the words, but it is important that there is a **pattern** or a **logic** to the grouping.

screaming	music	pleasure	pain
laughing	joy	fear	hope
dancing	running	agony	crashing
drinking	desperation	entertainment	happiness
eating	hopelessness	crying	shouting

(Note: there is more than one way of completing this exercise.)

2 When you have finished, working in groups, explain to each other the reasons for your groupings.

Order, order …

When you have quite a large amount of information it is important that you organise it so that you can bring some order to it.

3 Using work done both in your research and on the extracts you have studied, organise your information in order to respond to the following task:

From the information that you have, explain all the things you think contributed to the Titanic *disaster and also why it affected so many groups of people.*

You will see that there are two **key elements** required in your explanation:

All the things you think contributed to the Titanic *disaster*
and
why it affected so many groups of people.

If you take the first point then you might set down your **evidence** as in the table below:

The factors that contributed to the Titanic *disaster*	Reasons why this was so important / significant
One of the ice warnings did not get through to Captain Smith because he was in the à la carte restaurant, dining with passengers.	The captain may not have been aware of the severity of the weather conditions. If he had received this message, he might have taken a different course.

Can you see how you are beginning to build up **evidence** from which you can draw some conclusions?

Notice, also, that we are putting in a few **hypotheses** from the evidence given. It was a **fact** that the captain did not receive the ice warning. One **hypothesis** is that he may have taken a different course had he received it.

4   Now complete your organisation of evidence under the headings above.

5   Now pull together all your evidence under the heading:

Why it affected so many groups of people.

Use the format below to help you organise your ideas.

The groups of people it affected	Reasons why this group was affected by the disaster and the different ways they were affected.

Writing an explanation

At the start of this topic, we focused on the difference between fact and opinion. When you are writing, it is easy to express simple **facts**:

The lock on the door had been smashed.

When you give an **opinion**, you have to be a little more careful in your use of language. It would **not** be appropriate to write:

The lock on the door had been smashed by a large hammer

Unless you **know** this to be true. Instead, you should write:

The lock on the door had been smashed, perhaps by a large hammer or similar object.

The word *perhaps* is very important here. It is an **adverb**, referring to the verb *smashed*. Other words could equally have been used, such as *probably* or *possibly*, or different phrases such as *most likely*.

These are words or phrases that you use when you are **not certain** that something is true. They are very useful words, therefore, when you are forming a **hypothesis** from given facts.

6   In groups, spend five minutes brainstorming the different words or phrases that you could use to help you to express an **opinion** or **hypothesis**.

7   Now, using your evidence, your hypotheses and your adverbs that suggest theories, complete the task below, discussing each element in turn:

From the information that you have, explain all the things you think contributed to the *Titanic* disaster and also why it affected so many groups of people.

Check with the editor

8   When you have finished writing the first draft of your essay, swap your work with a partner and ask them to check for:
   • a range of evidence
   • interesting hypotheses
   • an answer to both parts of the question
   • use of words to signpost theories.

   Now redraft your work, using the suggestions for improvement made by your partner.

Writing assignment

Major task: you should spend about 40 minutes answering this question.

Your writing will be marked for:
- *how you structure and punctuate sentences (5 marks)*
- *how you organise paragraphs and ensure that the complete piece of writing hangs together (5 marks)*
- *the overall impact of your writing on the reader (15 marks)*
- *the accuracy of your spelling (5 marks)*

Read the short extract below, taken from the *Titanic Titanic!* website, which captures the dilemma of those passengers from the *Titanic* who had managed to get into a lifeboat.

Above the waves, nearly 1,500 people were now in the water, awaiting some kind of rescue. But although *Carpathia* was almost turning itself inside-out in the attempt to rescue them, those in the water would not survive for long. The water temperature was freezing, in the true sense of
5 the word, and many people would die from hypothermia well within the next hour, before any rescue could possibly arrive.

For those in the lifeboats, a dilemma on an unimaginable scale now faced them. Should they go back and make an effort to rescue some of those in the water, risking the boats from being swamped, and therefore putting
10 even more lives in danger? Or should they remain where they were, at a distance safe enough to stop anybody swamping the boat, but close enough to hear the dying screams of well over 1000 people?

History would provide us with the answer.

Now write a short piece entitled:

**The Titanic Ordeal
– A survivor's tale**

Imagine that this piece is for publication in a book collecting memories of the survivors to give them an idea about what it might have been like.

Your story should reflect the facts, but will also include some fictional details.

It is important to plan your ideas before you start to write. You could use a planning format like the one below:

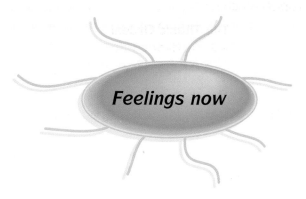

The Year 8 English test will help you and your teacher see how your reading and writing skills have developed since you took the test in Year 7. It will also show you which skills you are good at and where you need to be stronger, helping you to improve your skills for the SAT you will take at the end of Year 9, when you have completed Key Stage 3.

There are two test papers. One paper assesses your reading skills, and the other your writing skills. This section explains what is involved in each test, and what you have to do. It also provides:

- diagnostic tests, which show you where your strengths and weaknesses are, and what you need to do to improve your skills
- practice tests, which help you become familiar with the kind of texts, questions and timing you will meet in the actual tests, so that you will be fully prepared for them.

The reading paper

The texts

The reading paper may contain two, three or four pieces of text. They will come from a variety of text-types, such as:
- *an extract from a novel or short story*
- *a poem*
- *a piece of information text*
- *a piece of literary non-fiction, such as travel writing.*

The different texts will be linked by a theme or common subject, for example travel or families.

There will be an introduction to the texts, including information about:
- *the theme or subject that links the texts*
- *the source of each text – who wrote it and where it came from*
- *the background to the texts. This is particularly important if the text is a short extract from a longer text such as a novel or play.*

The questions

The reading paper contains questions that will test your reading skills, focusing on five key areas.

1 Identifying information or ideas and quoting from the text when required.

2 Working out meanings that are implicit. That means you have to read 'between the lines' of the text to work out what is meant. You will need to quote from the text when required.

3 Explaining the structure of texts, for example, how different parts relate to each other, or how the author has used grammar and different kinds of sentences to affect the meaning.

4 Commenting on the writer's choice and use of language.

5 Explaining the overall meaning and effect of a text, and how it affects you as a reader.

To test these skills in the reading paper, different types of questions are asked, including:

- questions that carry only 1 mark and require short answers. This type of question may:
  a) be multiple choice, where you simply tick your choice of answer
  b) ask you to copy a word or phrase from the text to show that you have understood its meaning
- questions that may be worth 2, 3, 4 or 5 marks.

The number of marks available and the space you are given for writing your answer will give you a clue as to how much time you should spend on a question. To help you, 5-mark questions will usually have a series of bullet points. Write about each bullet point to help you structure your answer and make sure it is complete.

Marks

The reading paper is worth 50 marks overall. These marks are divided between the five key reading skills explained above. Within the 50 marks, 10 are given to questions which test your grammatical understanding, for example, about the effects of different sentence structures, or how punctuation helps indicate the meaning in a text.

Giving the best answers to the questions

When answering questions on reading, it is important that you:

- **do exactly what you are asked.** For example, if you are told to copy something from the text, you will get no marks if you put it in your own words.
- **answer the question that is asked.** Make sure that you include only material that answers the question. Including any other material will waste your time, and will waste space in your answer book.
- **use textual detail whenever you are told.** Make sure you use direct quotations if you are commenting on language use or grammar.
- **respond to *all* the prompts** (such as bullet points) in a question, if any are given.
- **complete all the questions in the time allowed.** Plan your time carefully, but if you are running out of time, make sure that you attempt as many questions with high marks as you can.

Using your time carefully

The reading paper lasts for 1 hour and 15 minutes. In addition, you are given an extra 15 minutes to read through the texts before you look at the questions. Use the full 15 minutes reading time to get an overall idea of what the texts are about, and also to:

- think about the type of text each one is, and what that means. For example, how much expression of opinion does there seem to be in a non-fiction text?
- note anything you find difficult to understand so that you can return to it later
- identify striking or original examples of language use
- think about the effect each text has on you, and what causes the effect. For example, the subject-matter could shock you or the style of writing could be humorous and make you laugh.

The writing paper

The tasks

There are two questions on the writing paper:

- *the major task, which is worth 30 marks. It should take 40 minutes and your response should be detailed and wide-ranging; for example, a complete story, letter or article*
- *the minor task, which is worth 20 marks. It should take 25 minutes and be a shorter, more focused response, for example, just the opening of a story or a description of one place, person, or object.*

When marking your writing paper the marker will look for a number of different qualities. The major and minor tasks are marked slightly differently and the marker will look for different skills in each.

The major task

The four skills assessed in the major task are:

1 **How you structure and punctuate sentences.** For example, do you use full stops and capital letters, commas and other punctuation marks accurately? Do you vary your sentences so that they are not always simple (*The cat sat on the mat*), but are sometimes compound (*The cat sat on the mat and the dog entered the room.*) or complex (*As the dog entered the room, the cat was sitting on the mat*)? (Marks are given out of 5.)

2   **How you organise paragraphs and ensure that the complete piece of writing 'hangs together'**. For example, does a narrative follow a straightforward chronological sequence or, if you use a more complicated structure (such as flashback), does it make sense to the reader? If you are writing an argument, do your ideas follow a logical sequence so that the reader finds it hard to disagree with you? (Marks are given out of 5.)

3   **The overall impact of your writing on the reader.** This means how well your writing meets its **purpose** and how well it suits its **audience**. In other words, if it is a story, does it include interesting characters and believable events in a well-described setting? If it is a letter to a friend, have you used appropriate vocabulary and is the content interesting? (Marks are given out of 15.)

4   **The accuracy of your spelling**. You must show that you can spell difficult or less common words correctly to gain a high mark. (Marks are given out of 5.)

The minor task

The three skills assessed in the minor task are:

1   **Your choice and use of vocabulary**. You will gain more marks for using a wide vocabulary, even if you misspell some words. (Marks are given out of 4).

2   **How you structure and punctuate sentences and organise paragraphs**. See major task points 1 and 2 above. (Marks are given out of 4.)

3   **The overall impact of your writing on the reader**. See major task point 3 above. (Marks are given out of 12.)

Why are the major and minor tasks marked differently?

The reason for marking the major and minor tasks differently is because the two tasks ask you to do different things.

- You need to give a longer response to the major task. The marker will look separately at how you create sentences and organise paragraphs and how accurate your spelling is within this longer response.
- You need to give a shorter response to the minor task. Sometimes you will be asked to write only a few paragraphs, for example only three. This means that paragraph organisation is less important but your choice and use of vocabulary is more important.

Giving the best answers to questions

When answering writing questions, it is important that you:

- Write in the correct form. For example, if you are told to write a **description**, do not write a **story**.
- Write for the given reader. For example, if you are told to write one piece for a teenage friend and another for an unknown adult, you should use more formal language and grammar in the second piece.
- Cover the content. For example, if you are told to include certain information or events, or to start or finish in a given way, you will lose marks if you do not follow the instructions.
- Interest the reader. For example, use as wide a range of vocabulary as possible, and vary sentence structures and length of paragraphs.
- Show a high level of technical accuracy and neatness. For example, your work must be legible so that whoever is marking it can see that spellings and punctuation are accurate.

Using your time carefully

The time allowed for the writing paper is 1 hour and 15 minutes. You should spend:

- 40 minutes on the major task
- 25 on the minor task
- 10 minutes at the end, checking all your work for neatness, accuracy and completeness.

If you follow the guidance about how long to spend on each task, you will therefore have about 10 minutes left at the end to check your work for neatness, accuracy and completeness.

Each task is followed by a **planning frame** for you to copy out and make notes in – make sure you leave plenty of space in each of the boxes to write your ideas in. These frames will help you gather together and organise your ideas, and to begin to think about the best ways of writing about them. The planning frames are an extremely helpful part of the test, and you may find it helpful to allow the following time for planning and making notes:

- 10 minutes of your major task time
- 5–6 minutes of your minor task time.

Planning your writing will help you produce a piece of writing which is likely to be much better than if you simply start writing straight away.

Using the diagnostic and practice tests

The diagnostic tests

The diagnostic reading and writing tests on pages 130 and 134 will help you and your teacher to assess the strengths and weaknesses of your reading and writing skills. They are a slightly shorter and simpler version of the actual test. You may find it helpful to use this test quite near the start of Year 8 to assess how well you have remembered what you revised and learned in Year 7. The results from this test will give you and your teacher a better idea of areas that you need to work on to improve your reading and writing skills during Year 8.

The practice test

The practice reading and writing tests on pages 135 and 143 follow the exact format, length and timing of the actual test. You may find it helpful to use this test later in Year 8. The results will show you and your teacher where your reading and writing skills have improved during the year. It will also highlight specific areas of your reading and writing skills that might still be improved before you take the actual test.

Marking the tests and setting the targets

Your teacher will mark both the diagnostic tests and the practice tests. You will be given a total mark for each test:

- out of 60 marks for the diagnostic test
- out of 100 marks for the practice test.

Your teacher will be able to tell you a National Curriculum Level in English to which this mark corresponds. This will tell you how much overall progress you are making, as well as the progress in the separate areas of reading and writing, for which your teacher will give you a separate mark. Your teacher will even be able to give you a breakdown of your marks for all the different assessment focuses in reading and writing. This will show you exactly where your strengths and weaknesses are, and will focus on areas that will improve your reading and writing skills throughout Key Stage 3 and beyond.

Diagnostic tests

Reading test

Read the following texts:

The first text is taken from a collection of writing by scientists about food and drink. In it, Nicholas Kurti gives an account of the origins of one of the best-known modern convenience foods.

It is widely believed that Bird's custard is one of the earliest examples of 'convenience foods' or of regrettable substitutes designed purely to reduce the cost and the time of preparation of a dish. Nothing could be further from the truth. Indeed, the invention of Bird's custard is a shining
5   example of alleviating a deprivation caused by cruel nature.

Alfred Bird, whose father taught astronomy at Eton, was born in 1811 in Birmingham and in 1837 established himself as an analytical and retail pharmaceutical chemist there. When he married Elizabeth Lavinia Ragg he faced a challenge which was to influence his career. His young wife
10   suffered from a digestive disorder which prevented her from eating anything prepared with eggs or with yeast. But Elizabeth Lavinia was apparently yearning for custard to go with her favourite fruit pies so Alfred Bird started experimenting in his shop. The result was the custard powder bearing his name and based on cornflour, which when mixed with milk
15   produced, after heating, a sauce reminiscent in appearance, taste and consistency of a genuine egg-and-milk custard sauce.

The young wife was overjoyed and this substitute became the normal accompaniment to puddings at the Birds' dinner table, though, when they entertained, genuine custard sauce was offered to their guests. Then came
20   an occasion when, whether by accident or by design, 'Bird's custard' was served and Alfred must have been gratified to hear his guests declare it was the best custard they had ever tasted!

This then was the beginning of the firm Alfred Bird and Sons Ltd of Birmingham which for 120 years remained a family business, first under
25   the chairmanship of the founder, then of his son, Sir Alfred Bird Bt and then of his grandson Sir Robert Bird Bt. While the firm's main product remained custard powder Alfred Bird's other invention to circumvent his wife's digestive troubles, namely baking powder, was also manufactured and was used during the Crimean war so that British troops could be
30   given fresh, palatable bread.

Alfred Bird was a Fellow of the Chemical Society and, a few months after his death on 2 December 1878, a brief obituary was published in the *Journal of the Chemical Society*, Vol. 35, p.206, 1879. It described at some length Bird's interest in physics and meteorology, thus: 'He

35   constructed a beautiful set of harmonized glass bowls extending over 5 octaves which he used to play with much skill'; and 'in 1859 he constructed a water barometer with which he was fond of observing and showing to others the minute oscillations of the atmospheric pressure'. But of Bird's Custard Powder – not a word!

**The second text is an extract from Rukshana Smith's novel,
Salt on the Snow.** *Julie is watching her mum prepare an evening meal before they are joined by Julie's brother, Jim, and her dad.*

Dad worked the nightshift in an optics factory, so they always ate before he left. Julie went to help her mother prepare the evening meal. Pork chops were defrosting on the draining board, pink rivulets of blood running into the sink. She looked away in disgust.

5   'Mum,' she asked, 'have you ever thought of becoming a vegetarian?'

Mum tutted and put the chops under the grill. 'This isn't another of your phases, is it, Julie? I hoped you might have grown out of them by now!'

'Can you stop giving me meat, then,' Julie persisted. 'I wouldn't expect you to cook me anything special. I'm quite happy with potatoes and
10   vegetables.'

'Hm, that would go down well, wouldn't it?' Mum retorted with unusual vigour. 'You need meat with your pale skin and red hair, you're just the type to get anaemia. It says so in my magazines. You've got to get your protein. You know your father likes to have meat once a day. It makes him
15   feel good.' She wiped her hands on a towel, leaving a faint bloodstain.

'It doesn't make *me* feel good,' Julie snapped, looking at the pink streak. 'Meat is full of hormones and additives, we're all being poisoned.'

'That's enough now,' Mum scolded tartly. 'Go and lay the table, and stop being so difficult.'

20   Dad came down and switched on the television. As soon as Jim returned Mum served up, and a smell of boiled cabbage soured the air. Behind her father's head, in the corner of the room, pictures of famine victims rolled across the screen.

'I saw an ad for a volunteer agency today,' Julie remarked. 'I thought I
25   might find out about it. They're asking for helpers to get old people's shopping.'

Dad looked up, his mouth full. 'Do-gooders!' he scoffed. 'Charity work! You know I don't hold with that sort of thing.' A bit of meat flew out of his mouth, landing on the bottle of ketchup.

30   'Don't upset yourself, Jack,' soothed his wife, pouring him a cup of tea. 'You'll give yourself indigestion.'

'But I ask you, Margaret, charity work!' He made it sound like murder. 'It's no use spoonfeeding people, they ought to help themselves. That's what's wrong with this country. Full of scroungers and layabouts.'

35   Julie forced down a mouthful of rubbery pork, trying to keep calm.

Now answer these questions.

Questions 1–7 are on **Bird's Custard: The True Story**

1   **(a)** In the first paragraph, what does the writer's attitude
               towards 'convenience foods' seem to be?

                                                                          [2 marks]

     (b) Find and copy an adjective in the first sentence which
               helps to convey this attitude.

                                                                          [1 mark]

2   What sort of shop did Alfred Bird own?

                                                                          [1 mark]

3   What does the word *yearning* (line 12) suggest about
     Elizabeth Lavinia's personality?

                                                                          [1 mark]

4   Look again at the last sentence of the third paragraph (*Then
     came an occasion ... they had ever tasted*). Comment on how
     the structure and punctuation help to convey the meaning.

                                                                          [3 marks]

5   *Bt.* (line 25) is an abbreviation for Baronet, a title like *Lord* or
     Sir. Find and copy another abbreviation in this text and write
     out the full version of the word.

                                                                          [1 mark]

6   Explain the use of the dash and the exclamation mark in the
     final sentence of this text.

                                                                          [2 marks]

7   What do you think is the writer's attitude towards Alfred Bird?
     You should write about:
     • the details about Bird's life he chooses to include
     • the comments he adds
     • his choice of words and use of sentence structures.

                                                                          [5 marks]

Questions 8–12 are on the extract from **Salt on the Snow**

8 What does the phrase *Mum retorted with unusual vigour* (lines 11–12) suggest that she is usually like?

[2 marks]

9 (a) What atmosphere is created by the verbs *tutted* (line 6) and *snapped* (line 16)?

[1 mark]

(b) Find and copy **two** other verbs which contribute to creating the same atmosphere later in the text.

[2 marks]

10 What is the effect of the word *soured* in line 21?

[2 marks]

11 Why does Julie's Dad object to charity work?

[2 marks]

12 Explain how the reader of this text is made to share Julie's feelings of disgust at eating meat. You should write about:
- her parents' comments and actions
- how she sees the pork chops
- the writer's choice of language.

[5 marks]

Writing test

Think back to the texts you read about Bird's Custard and the rather tense meal in Julie's house. Food is an important feature in most people's lives, and can generate strong feelings, for example about hunger and poverty, about genetically modified crops or about food fashions.

Write a story about a group of people having a meal together. During the meal, an argument begins on a subject connected with food. Your writing should entertain the reader while also exploring some of the issues raised by the argument.

Before starting to plan, you will need to decide:

- who are the people at the meal? Is it a family, or a group of friends, for example? Are they from similar or different backgrounds?
- what is the issue they are arguing about? Is it very serious, or does it have a funny side? How many different viewpoints are there? Does somebody 'win' the argument?

Remember you are writing a story, not a piece of persuasive writing: this is a piece which should explore, imagine and entertain. Before starting to write, you will need to think about:

- the choice of language which will help your reader picture the scene and understand something about the people involved
- how you will structure your writing – for example, will you write a third-person narrative, or will you write in the first person?

Copy the planning grid below to help you organise your ideas. Don't forget to leave plenty of space to write your ideas in the boxes.

What the argument is about/how it begins:		
People involved	What s/he is like	Their views
How the argument ends:		

[30 marks]

Practice tests

Reading test: Machines

> **REMEMBER:**
> - *The test is 1 hour 15 minutes long, plus 15 minutes' reading time.*
> - *You therefore have 15 minutes to read the texts before answering the questions that follow them.*
> - *There are different types of questions. The spaces for answers and the number of marks indicate how much you need to write.*
> - *Ask your teacher if you are not sure what to do.*

Introduction

We live in an age which loves machines and gadgets. Many of the jobs we do would be very tedious without the help of machines. Nowadays, advances in computing and electronics mean that an astonishing range of complicated, accurate procedures can be completed at just the push of a button. Two of the texts here are about earlier times. The first describes a time when machines created a sense of awe. The second shows how the lack of safety procedures in factories could make them very dangerous places indeed. The last text is addressed to present-day readers who are interested in buying a computer for home or business use.

Portrait of a Machine

This is a poem by Louis Untermeyer. He was born at the end of the nineteenth century, and was particularly impressed by the technological advances made in the early part of his life.

Accident at the Croft

This is an extract from *A Roof Over Your Head*, a novel by Bill Naughton. The novel is set in the mid-twentieth century, in a Lancashire cotton mill. It is about the hardships suffered at work and at home by the people whose lives were ruled by the factory.

How we can help you

This is part of an advertising leaflet for PC World. It tells customers about the support they can expect if they choose to shop at PC World for home or business computers and then run into problems when they use the equipment.

Portrait of a Machine

> In this poem, Louis Untermeyer describes the beauty he sees in a great machine. Although he admires it, he also sees something sinister in the relationship between man and machine.

What nudity as beautiful as this
Obedient monster purring at its toil;
Those naked iron muscles dripping oil,
And the sure-fingered rods that never miss?
5 This long and shining flank of metal is
Magic that greasy labour cannot spoil;
While this vast engine that could rend the soil
Conceals its fury with a gentle hiss.

It does not vent its loathing, it does not turn
10 Upon its makers with destroying hate.
It bears a deeper malice; lives to earn
Its master's bread and laughs to see this great
Lord of the earth, who rules but cannot learn,
Become the slave of what his slaves create.

Accident at the Croft

> The narrator and Tom are both at work in the machine shop of a cotton mill. The workers in the factory are only allowed a break for one reason: to go to the toilet. Many of them take this as a chance for a quick smoke while they are out – which is strictly forbidden. Tom does not smoke, but because the work is so hard, his mother gives him a great pile of jam sandwiches to eat every day. When he 'goes to the toilet', Tom eats some of his sandwiches, then smuggles more back into the machine shop under his overalls. When this extract begins, Tom's mind is perhaps more on his sandwiches than on the machine he should be operating . . .

One morning Tom goes out and nips back with some bread and jam. We have the machines running in their order, and my mind is down to the job, hurrying about, watching the small points, taking no notice of anything but what I'm working on, when a fearful screaming breaks out. I rush to the
5 side of the next machine. It is Tom. The machine has taken his hand. The two massive iron rollers have drawn together. He has been coaxing the yarn to a final smoothness, as the machine is tightening up. He is used to it; thousands of times he has done the same. He draws back . . . . But this terrible moment he is too late. His whole hand has been taken round.
10 Crushed in the tremendous iron pressure of the rollers, and carried to the caustic tank.

One long, awful cry is coming from Tom. His mouth wide agape. I can see a chewed morsel of bread and jam lying in it. The machine is running on indifferently.

15 'Oh, Tom, Tom . . .' I moan. I fall upon the big handle. The wide driving belt slurs off slow and stubbornly. From me comes the prayer of my infant days: 'Hail, Holy Queen, Mother of Mercy! Hail, Holy Queen, Mother of Mercy!'

The men from all over the shop are around us now. They are all so different: their faces are white and have feelings on them. They recklessly
20 tear and drag the machine to reverse. It is slow, the way it turns back. The big wheels, the ugly cogs, and the cruel rollers – they will not release Tom's hand. I am beside him. The men have their arms around him. He is roaring in agony: 'Oh get me out! Get me out! I'm burning!' His hand is deep in the caustic tank.

25 And then I see it brought away – Tom's hand. A ghastly mess of pulpy bone and flesh is Tom's young hand. 'For Christ's sake, faint!' appeals one of the men, Johnny. But Tom doesn't faint. He is of old Lancashire stock, a tough-natured breed. He shakes his head, as though he would spare this commotion; then turns to me, with some of his old voice: 'I'm dry. Gerrus
30 a drink of watter, Bill.'

Johnny covers the hand with a red dinner hanky. Tom makes a gulp at the water. Three of us walk up the slope beside him. One has gone to call the ambulance. Mr Owner has sent word he will take Tom to hospital in his car. At this Tom grins: 'Crikey! I'm gunna have a ride in t'gaffer's car!'

35 It was raining. Mr Owner met us, and put his arm on Tom, in fatherly anxiety. He hurried to the driving seat. We were just helping Tom into the back of the car when Mr Owner stopped us. 'Just a minute, one of you had better find a few sacks to put on the floor and seats in case his blood drips.' Tom waited in the rain, one foot on the car step, until I got back
40 with the sacks. Mr Owner told me how to spread them out.

It was reasonable enough not to wish his car to be blood-messed for the sake of a minute. But the men, they spoke their hate and contempt of Mr Owner more over that small act than for all he ever did against them.

When I saw Tom again his arm came to a pointed end near the wrist. He had
45 grown from the rest in hospital. He shouted a lot, and he swore much worse.

I don't know what his thoughts were.

From **A Roof Over Your Head** by Bill Naughton

How we can help you

PC World is a well known chain of computer superstores. This advertising leaflet is designed to tell the customer about the advantages of using PC World as their computer supplier. If anything goes wrong, there are many ways to get help and advice.

How **we** can help you

I'm having problems with my product, where do I get help?..

FOR MOST PORTABLE PRODUCTS

Just return the product to your local store or phone them for further details on what to do next. The number of the store where you bought the product is on your receipt.

FOR MOBILE PHONES CALL | **0870 909 0550**

FOR CAMCORDERS CALL | **0870 909 0559**

FOR PCS, PRINTERS & LAPTOPS
www.pcservicecall.co.uk

Our Website, has solutions for most common problems experienced by our customers, or just email us at
support@pcservicecall.co.uk

OR PHONE THE PC SET-UP HELPLINE
0906 752 5600

(Calls charged at 75p per minute, maximum call duration 20 minutes.) **Lines open 24 hours a day, 365 days a year.**

> **Did you know, over 80% of problems are set-up or software related and can be solved over the phone?**

Our PC Set-up Helpline is available **24 hours a day** to help you rectify any set-up or software related problems, which are not covered under your manufacturer's warranty. Our technicians are trained to help you by diagnosing and fixing your problem over the telephone to get you back up and running fast!

...with you every step of the way

How **we** can help you

I'm having problems running software, what do I do?

Call PC SoftwareCall | **0906 559 7897**

(Calls charged at £1 per minute, maximum call duration 20 minutes, average call length 6 minutes.) **Lines open 24 hours a day, 365 days a year.**
Our experts can help you with:

* How to load games and other software.
* Downloading games from the Internet.
* Configuring your hardware for gaming.
* Gaming on line.
* Much, much more!

I'm having problems using the Internet?

Call PC InternetCall | **0906 553 1556**

(Calls charged at £1 per minute, maximum call duration 20 minutes.) **Lines open 24 hours a day, 365 days a year.**
Our experts can help you with:

* How to use search engines & bookmark your favourite sites.
* Setting up parental controls.
* Creating your own web page.
* Recommendations on the best sites to visit...and much more!

Or with business applications?

Call PC BusinessCall | **0906 553 1557**

(Calls charged at £1 per minute, maximum call duration 20 minutes.) Lines open 8am-8pm Monday to Friday (excluding Bank Holidays).
Call our experts for advice on:

* Microsoft operating systems.
* Microsoft Office.
* Lotus SmartSuite.
* Linux...and much more!

...with you every step of the way

Questions 1–6 are on **Portrait of a Machine**

1   In the first line of the poem, the writer describes the machine as *beautiful*. Find and copy from the first stanza another word which conveys a similar reaction.

[1 mark]

2   Look again at the last two lines of the first stanza. What do they suggest about the machine?

[3 marks]

3   Why do you think the writer has split this poem into two stanzas?

[2 marks]

4   What do you think the writer means by the last three lines of the poem, which say that the machine:

> *Laughs to see this great*
> *Lord of the earth, who rules but cannot learn,*
> *Become the slave of what his slaves create.*

[2 marks]

5   Comment on the writer's use of the semi-colon in this poem.

[2 marks]

6   Explain how the writer's use of language makes the machine sound human, and the effect this has on you.
You should write about:

- the meaning of particular words and images
- what the writer seems to feel about the machine
- how you react to the ideas in the poem.

[5 marks]

Questions 7–15 are on **Accident at the Croft**

7   What does the machine described in the first paragraph do?

[1 mark]

8   The accident happens because Tom:
    (a) is not very skilful
    (b) is not concentrating
    (c) follows the wrong procedure
    (d) allows the yarn to catch his hand.

[1 mark]

9   Comment on the structure and effect of the last sentence in
    the first paragraph: *Crushed in the tremendous iron pressure
    of the rollers, and carried to the caustic tank.*

[2 marks]

10   In the last sentence of the second paragraph, what does the
    adverb *indifferently* describe? What is the effect of this? Find
    and copy an adjective from the fourth paragraph which adds
    to this effect.

[3 marks]

11   How are the seriousness and the extent of the injury to
    Tom's hand conveyed through the language used in the
    second sentence of paragraph 5?

[2 marks]

12   Why do you think Johnny covered Tom's hand with a red
    handkerchief?

[2 marks]

13   Tom's workmates are upset when Mr Owner is bothered about
    Tom's blood spoiling the car. Apart from that incident, do you
    think the men like Mr Owner? Find and copy a phrase from
    the text to support your decision.

[2 marks]

14   What is the effect of using the present tense in this narrative?

[2 marks]

15   At the end of this text, the storyteller writes *I don't know what
    his thoughts were*. What do you think Tom's thoughts would
    be as he looks back on this incident several years later?
    You should write about:
    ● how he remembers the accident happening
    ● the reaction of his workmates
    ● what Mr Owner did
    ● how the accident has changed him.

[5 marks]

Questions 16–20 are on **How can we help you**

16 You have bought a computer from PC World and are having problems running business applications on it. On which days can you **not** get advice from the PC World BusinessCall line?

[1 mark]

17 Complete the following table to explain **four** ways in which the presentation of the leaflet is intended to be helpful to the reader. An example has been done for you.

Feature	Explanation
Arrow at top of left-hand page	Guides your eye to the information

[4 marks]

18 Why do you think a header and footer are used on these pages? Give **two** reasons.

[2 marks]

19 Complete the following table by picking out three words or short phrases from the text and explaining how they make the reader feel reassured that she/he will be well looked-after by PC World in the event of any computer problems.

Word or short phrase	How it reassures the reader

[3 marks]

20 Imagine you were thinking of buying a computer from PC World. Explain how successful this text would be, and why, in persuading you that PC World would help you solve any problems you might encounter.

[5 marks]

Writing test: Machines

> **Major task:** you should spend about 40 minutes answering this question.

March of the Machines!

It is the time that the human race has dreaded ... the time when their own creations have turned on them ... the time when machines have developed minds of their own and cannot be controlled. What will this mean? Where will it end? Can anything be done to save the world?

Write a story about the world taken over by machines.

> **REMEMBER TO INCLUDE IN YOUR NARRATIVE:**
> - *descriptions of places, people, ideas, etc.*
> - *dialogue, if appropriate*
> - *a central event, which is the focus of the story.*

[30 marks]

Planning

Before you begin to write your story, copy this frame and use it to gather together and organise your ideas. Don't forget to leave enough space in each of the boxes to include your ideas.

March of the Machines! – planning frame

Main idea of the story: what happens?		
How is it resolved?		
What atmosphere are you trying to create?		
Characters in the story (humans and machines)	What they are like – how to describe them	What they do – their importance to the story
Places in the story	Descriptive details of places	What happens there
Notes on the content/structure of the story		
How to begin	The middle	How to end

Minor task: you should spend about 25 minutes answering this question.

User review

These days, most of us use all kinds of household equipment and technology to make our lives easier, or to entertain us: microwaves, home computers, DVD players, etc. When you want to buy something like this for the first time – or when you want to replace an outdated or broken item – it can be really difficult to decide what is the best buy. Magazines and newspapers often contain reviews or comparisons of equipment to help you make up your mind.

Write a review of a piece of household equipment or entertainment technology that you know about and have used. Write <u>three paragraphs</u>: the first should describe what the item is and what it does; the second should comment on how easy it is to use and how well it does its job; the third should sum up whether you would recommend this item or not, and your reasons why.

> **REMEMBER TO INCLUDE IN YOUR NARRATIVE:**
> * *choose an item with which you are familiar.*
> * *write your review for someone who is not an expert*
> * *make your recommendation clear.*

[20 marks]

Planning

Before you begin to write your review, copy this frame and use it to gather together and organise your ideas. Don't forget to leave enough space in each of the boxes to include your ideas.

User review: – planning frame

Item chosen:
Paragraph 1 – what is it and what does it do?
Paragraph 2 – how easy is it to use? How well does it do its job?
Paragraph 3 – Would you recommend this item or not? Reasons?